DON'T NEVER SAY CAIN'T

DON'T
NEVER SAY CAIN'T

Ethel Strainchamps

DOUBLEDAY & COMPANY, INC., GARDEN CITY, NEW YORK

1

CAUTION: NARROW TUNNEL AHEAD

During my first year in college I began having two recurrent dreams. In one dream I was laboriously climbing a rickety ladder, or makeshift staircase, which was built of flimsy, narrow boards tacked to a frame that stood parallel to a high wall and ended in a small dark opening at the juncture of the wall and the ceiling. At the start of the dream I was always more than halfway up the ladder and was climbing doggedly on, in spite of an almost paralyzing dread of having to crawl through a narrow tunnel that I knew I was going to have to negotiate when I got to the top. Retreat was impossible. About two out of every three rungs of the ladder were giving way beneath me as I climbed.

I never did get quite to the top of the ladder in the dream, but the dread of having to squeeze through that tunnel ahead, to emerge into God knew what, was so acute that it would stay with me after I awoke, and, though I have never had a conscious sensation of claustrophobia, I learned from that dream what it is like.

In the other dream, I was in some sort of academic hall, searching anxiously for a classroom that I had never been in before. It was near the end of the term, and I had just discovered that there was a class on my schedule that I had overlooked. It seemed that the class was just then convening for the day, and that, as I searched for the room, I was also having to make a crucial decision: whether to join the class and subject myself to the bewilderment of listening to unintelligible lectures and the risk of failing the impending exam, or to go on missing the class and accept the failure without the risk.

In that dream too I felt that I was doomed to have to face the worst of the possible consequences—that I *was* going to enter the class and that I *would* be baffled and overwhelmed. In the meanwhile, I was wandering in a daze of anxiety, despair, and remorse, but remorse—for having negligently missed the opportunity to learn something I would have to know—was uppermost. I always awoke before I found the classroom, which proved to be as elusive as it was threatening, but I acquired from that dream a lifelong empathy with the class dunce.

To an analyst of dreams, those two would probably seem to be loaded with symbolism, but the states of mind they induced in me were so familiar that the dreams only seemed to me to be small, unsubtle dramatizations of my chief waking concerns. I took the ladder dream as a clear warning against excessive ambition, though it never occurred to me to wonder about the significance of the tunnel. The other (visible) physical properties were so familiar and so unchanging that I often suspected that the dream was a re-run of an actual memory. I did dimly recall having made some rather scary climbs into lofts and attics in my earliest childhood, but none of those had ended in anything very frightening at the top. The only terrifying thing I remembered happening to me in a loft was that once, when I was four, I fell, swathed in hay, through a hole in the floor into the horses' manger. The fall didn't hurt me but I screamed in fright a few seconds after I had landed when it dawned upon me that the horse within whose reach I had fallen had not noticed anything peculiar about the gob of hay I sat half-buried in. It just went munching obliviously on, and I fully expected to be the next thing to go. But that fear, while intense for the moment, did not linger, and I'm sure it left no scars. That tunnel in my dream had its source in something deeper, something an analyst might recognize, I suppose, as a fear of death, a dread of the unknown, or even the memory of being born.

The second dream left me with only an intensification of the chronic anxiety I felt that I would fail to do something I had to do to achieve my true goal, which was nothing less than to qualify for the company of the sages by learning everything there was to know.

I think it was the splitting of the atom that cured me of having both nightmares. Anyway, I stopped having them at about the same time I finally faced the fact that I was never going to learn anything about atomic physics. Once I had accepted that defeat, I was able to close my mind to one field of knowledge after another with no regrets and no feeling of guilt, and the dreams stopped recurring.

(By then, also, a few of my magazine pieces had been published in college anthologies—some of them as examples of good writing—and a few noted linguists and lexicographers had admitted me into their inner circles. But I would rather not believe that my subconscious had been lulled into quiescence by those minor achievements.)

I first got the delusion of potential omniscience when I was five and was first starting to school. No one in my family had gone beyond the third grade, but in the one-room school I attended there were several upper-grade students, and I got the notion from listening to them recite that the answers to all questions were written down in books, and that being able to know everything was a simple matter of learning to read better.

I had taught myself to read simple material before I started to school, without using books. I first learned the words on food containers—*salt, pepper, sugar, flour,* and *vinegar* were among the first words in my reading vocabulary, and *reg us pat off* was among the first phrases. That phrase, an abbreviation of "registered U. S. patent office," was then printed on every container of trade-named food or medicine, but its meaninglessness as I read it didn't disturb me particularly. From what I had seen of written language up to then, I was willing to assume that there was an infinite number of words and phrases in it that were meaningless to me, though I was determined to reduce that number as soon as possible.

At that time, we had only two books in our house—the Holy Bible and *The ABC and XYZ of Bee Culture,* both of which my father used in pursuit of his two chief hobbies; he was an apiarist and an atheist. He also took two related periodicals—the *American Bee Journal,* a monthly, and the *Appeal to Reason,* a Socialist weekly. I could read only the titles of the two books, but I was already reading the headlines, the picture captions, and the ads in the two periodicals before I started to school. In fact I had already extended my innate skepticism to include the printed word by that time as the result of reading two ads in my father's revered political weekly. To my consternation, the first ad commanded *"Don't Wear a Truss,"* and, just as I had resolved never to do so, I turned the page and got contrary instructions from a truss manufacturer.

At home, my predilection for reading had been regarded as an unfortunate and reprehensible addiction, so it came as a delightful surprise to me that in school the habit was looked on with favor. From the first grade on, oral speed-reading was my forte, and my teachers were duly impressed. Their method of teaching reading —if it can be called a method—was to teach you the letters of the alphabet, then give you a book and tell you to begin reading orally. If you couldn't do so, they told you the words one by one, and then had you go back and put them together to make a sentence. With several other grades to teach, they had no time for refinements of this system, and in truth it seemed to work well enough. At least I don't remember any pupil in any of the four one-room schools I attended before I was in the fifth grade who couldn't read at all.

In spite of the fact that I found recitations by the more advanced students so enthralling that I never took time to look at my own reading assignments ahead of time, I was able to maintain my record as fastest reader, no mistakes, until I was finally stumped in the third grade because of the limitations of my speaking vocabulary. What threw me was the word *perhaps,* one that I had never heard used. I made a quick, on-the-spot guess that the strange word was the written version of *a purpose* and I called it *perups,* a kind of transposition of the sounds of my native tongue that I had come to expect in books. The words I knew as *hunderd, larnyx, perty, irrevelant, cupalo,* and *apern* underwent the same sort of transposition in print, I had noticed. In fact, I had by that time picked up the notion that there was not necessarily much connection between the way teachers expected you to pronounce words in oral reading and the way they were pronounced in real life.

Teacher speech in general struck me as a special lingo, lying somewhere between book language and normal speech. I was willing to adopt it myself for use in the schoolroom, but I had no reason to believe that it was ever spoken elsewhere. In fact I felt so strongly that it was inappropriate for everyday use that when one of my step-uncles brought his ex-schoolteacher wife back to the hills from Colorado, I helpfully taught their three children to abandon some of their teacherish speech habits.

I remember one puzzling episode in Aunt Elda's kitchen when I was visiting there shortly after I had started to school. Aunt Elda was fixing her children and me a snack, and she handed Marjorie two pieces of bread and jelly, asking her to take one to her brother.

Marjorie said, "He doesn't want any."

I said, "What do you say it like that for? That ain't the way people says it."

"That isn't the way people *say* it," Aunt Elda, who had resumed her chores, said distractedly.

"That's what I told her," I said.

(Aunt Elda had a mental breakdown within the next year and had to be sent away to Nevada. I am beginning now to understand why.)

I found *isn't, doesn't,* and *those* particularly irritating to the ear, probably because of their unpleasant z sounds. Aunt Elda kept telling us that her children were right and I was wrong, but my influence was reinforced by everybody else's practice and soon prevailed.

My father was my model of speech propriety. He was always deferred to by our neighbors as a man of superior learning, especially after we moved to Newton County from the somewhat less rustic Missouri-Ozarks county where I was born. Like the neighbors, he was a hillman and farmer, from an unbroken line of hillmen and farmers. But he was also a trained carpenter who could use a slide rule and who could figure roof angles by using geometry and he was a scientific beekeeper who used hives and pedigreed queens instead of beegums and local stock. His musical talents and social graces lent him additional prestige. He could play the fiddle and the parlor organ by notes, and could sing all the old songs—folk songs, hymns, ballads—either solo, accompanying himself on the organ, or supplying a confident bass in group singing.

Before we moved from my native Polk County, he used to act as host to singings at our house. These were attended by men only, and I usually went to bed before the affairs got much more than started, but, from hearing my father practicing them around the house, I learned all four parts to most of the songs and I could line out any one of them, either by itself or in harmony with as many of the other three parts as anyone chose to join me with. In Newton County, where the culture seemed to be somewhat less advanced and the morals somewhat looser, my father often lent his social talents to arranging square dances at our house. He would sell hand-numbered tickets to the young people in the neighborhood, the proceeds going to the caller and to the extrafamilial musicians. He contributed his own services as fiddler and mine as the seconder on the organ. In that function, from the time I was seven on and my older half-sisters preferred to dance, I assisted the musicians at our dances by pounding out chords in rhythm on the organ, as my father had taught me to do. Once you learned the three changes for all the keys, the only trick was in sensing when to switch from one to the other. (I was considered a musical prodigy at the time, but I never did learn any more about music than I knew then—how to harmonize and when to change keys.) Our dances were always well attended, and by orderly, if exuberant, groups. A strict teetotaler himself, my father would permit no imbibing of spirits on the premises, and if some young man showed up obviously under the influence, Papa always got him to leave by merely making a polite request, such was the authority of his manner.

My father's appearance and manner of dress also set him somewhat apart from the neighbors. He could do hard labor—felling trees, driving posts, pounding up rocks —with the most rugged of them in spite of his age. (He was forty-five when I was born.) But he was slight of build; had fine black hair which he kept neatly combed and parted; he looked mildly at the world from soft, intelligent brown eyes; and he wore a mustache which was naturally auburn and bushy but which he trimmed and tinted with Brownatone every Sunday morning in front of the mirror over the kitchen washstand. Instead of the usual blue denim overalls and workshirts, he wore corduroy trousers, tucked into boots, and khaki shirts.

My father stood out, in short, as a man of exceptional refinement and cultural attainments, and I had no reason to suspect that his manners, including his style of speech, would not be acceptable in cultivated circles anywhere. He was even rather strict about certain niceties of grammar and pronunciation. He objected to the word *hain't* and to certain double negatives; if he heard one of us say, "I hain't got nary un," he made us correct it to "I ain't got ary un." I caught on to the nature of the double-negative taboo very early, and this led to a routine exchange between Blanche, the daredevil of the family, and me, the most cowardly member. Leading the way higher up into a tree, or farther out into deep water, or across the creek by way of a small shaky log, Blanche would toss out the admonition, "Don't never say cain't!" I would nevertheless usually hang back, at least gaining time while I made the feeble rejoinder, "Don't ever say 'don't never.'" I was well aware of the moral superiority of her line, though, and in the end it had more effect on me than mine did on her, I trust.

My father also frowned on our pronouncing *are* as "air" and *it* as "hit." Persuaded that a few such solecisms were marks of ignorance, we naturally regarded ourselves as socially superior to the neighbors who used them, and I supposed that, when I had learned to speak well enough to pass muster with my father, I was using the kind of English that all educated speakers of the language used in real life, though I was well aware that it was not the same as the language used in books. That I regarded as a kind of artificial language used *only* in books and in schoolrooms.

Nevertheless, by the time I had finished elementary school, I had learned to pronounce it well enough to retain my rank as oral-reading champion and to write it well enough that I was already being encouraged by my teachers to think of myself as a born book author. Then when I started to Joplin High School and first heard the urban middle-class dialect all around me, I jumped to the startling conclusion that I had moved into a world where book English was the everyday language.

Thanks to my extensive reading and to a natural facility for languages, I was able to effect the switch almost immediately, though I made the usual beginner's mistake of overcorrection at first. I began, for example, to say "you" for "you'uns," "potato" for "putater," and "kind of" for "kindy." Then I discovered that what my classmates were really saying was "y'all," "putata," and "kinda." Furthermore, I soon noticed that my new associates looked at me strangely when I said I had dissuaded somebody when I meant I had talked him out of something, and even when I used such common book words as "inevitable" and "tantamount."

Since my sole purpose in changing dialects was to keep from being conspicuous, I soon backed up considerably, but when I did I lost the pleasant illusion that by abandoning my native dialect I was abandoning error for truth. I began to say "lonjeray" and "exKWIZit," pronunciations I knew were not then in the dictionary, but only with a distinct loss in self-respect and in the full consciousness that I was engaged in mere social climbing. I still believed then that Webster's unabridged dictionary, a copy of which my father had inherited from his father when I was nine, contained the revealed truth about words as they were used in books and schoolrooms, and I flouted its dicta only with a certain amount of corrupting cynicism.

The linguists say that nobody switches from one dialect to another of his native language without a desire to repudiate his origins, but if that was my reason, I kept it well disguised from myself. I thought I was making a temporary and superficial adaptation to circumstances, as you would don native garb in a foreign country to keep from attracting attention. I still thought that my kind of people were the best kind, and that no deep, honest feelings could be expressed except in their kind of language. And now I wonder if I have ever really changed my mind; now I wonder if my using an acquired language for all of my adult life has not given me the illusion that I have only been playing at living for all those years.

When I first read that linguistic theory about the reason people elect to change dialects, I felt a pang of regret for what my choice must have done to my father. I realized then that he had intuitively arrived at the same conclusion, and that he believed I was deliberately rejecting my family and its way of life when I chose to leave home to get an education. That he had forgiven me unreservedly and had loved me no less for my waywardness only made me feel guiltier in retrospect. I was the only one of the eleven children he had fathered by three successive wives who abandoned our native milieu and its habits and folkways, but he always treated us all with equal tenderness and regard.

The real reasons for my break with my origins were not clear to me at the time, and they still aren't, though I never thought that I was taking a particularly admirable course. And, fortunately, I never did confuse intellectual advancement, which was what I was seeking in high school, with social advancement. My early perception of the irrelevance of intellectual attainments to social status spared me much fruitless striving then and disillusionment later. Without any previous exposure to a class other than my own—at the bottom of the social scale—I already understood and accepted the fact of class divisions, probably from having perceived it in books. My

precocious lack of concern about the matter was probably
due to my view of myself even then as a writer, and
hence as a person who was outside class divisions.

Of course I wouldn't have enjoyed being either
snubbed or patronized by my classmates, so I tried to
keep entirely to myself to avoid both. It turned out that
my chief difficulty was in keeping my intellectual peers
at the social distance that I saw would be most con-
venient for both them and me. My easy acquisition of
their manners and speechways, along with the fact that
I was soon joining them on the honor roll, the staff of the
school paper, and the debate teams, was always mislead-
ing some of them as to my true social place, and creating
embarrassing contretemps.

This confusion was aggravated by the circumstance
that I rode home on the streetcar with some of them—
toward the same exclusive residential section. What they
didn't know was that I had to go in by the back door of
the house I lived in, or that I ate in the kitchen and slept
in the maid's room. In my out-of-school hours I was earn-
ing my board and room and my expense money by doing
housework, an occupation that none of my classmates
could have considered as being any drearier or more
demeaning than I did.

My first awkward social contretemps occurred in gym
class one day, when Mary Anne Calbert, with whom I
had been paired at the tall end of the class and with
whom I shared a facility in Alfalfa, the currently popular
language game, suddenly said brightly, "Milefy mulfuther
and dalfad knowlfow your mulfuther and dalfad."

A jarring vision of her sleek and proper parents in the
company of my fat, illiterate stepmother and my un-
sophisticated father left me speechless.

"Your father *is* Dr. Reed, isn't he?" she said, naming a doctor in the neighborhood who was so rich and snobbish that it was assumed he sent his children to private schools; nobody knew their names or what they looked like.

"Oh no. That's another Reed," I said, and hastily changed the subject.

Shortly after that I had one experience with out-and-out dissembling on the matter of my social status, with such discomfiting consequences that I was never tempted to repeat it. The couple I lied to were taking me home one night after a debate on the League of Nations, which my colleague and I had won. The husband, a lawyer from Carthage, was a judge in the tournament and he stopped to compliment me after the debate, then offered to take me home. He and his wife were both expensively dressed and he was driving a large, new Cadillac. On the way home he talked with me intelligently about the League, then he commented, as we reached my employers' neighborhood, that it was unusual for a girl with my social background to be interested in debating, in the first place, and, in the second place, to hold such liberal views. He concluded that he regarded me as a credit to our class —meaning his and mine—and he congratulated himself for having been such an astute debating judge.

I felt compelled to correct his misconception but I preferred to spare him the shock of the whole sensational truth, so I said something about a relative of mine who was a relative of my employers', leaving the impression, I hoped, that I was no more than a poor relation, once removed, whom they were befriending. He tried to pin me down, asking me, among other things, the name of the family I lived with. I had to tell him that, but I was evasive about everything else. Since the two couples lived some miles apart, I didn't expect the lie to get back to my employers, but it was not more than three days later that they confronted me with it. They had run into the friendly couple the night before at a party, and of course I was the topic of their first remarks. Not knowing anything then about cocktail-party conversations, I was disgusted with them all for having had nothing more elevating to talk about, but I was also horribly contrite at having lied. I was only amazed that my employers were not more indignant about it than they were.

Mary Anne, my gym class partner, eventually found out the truth about my situation, and then she started coming over to help me with the dishes after dinner so we could study together later. But she was an exception. Most of my classmates, as I had foreseen, found such an adjustment beyond them. Even adults, including some of those who know me well now, find it hard to accept the fact that a person—and especially a person of my sex— who is indistinguishable from them by any of the common caste marks, could ever have been totally déclassée. This mental block is probably due to the fact that there are few, if any, models of the socially self-metamorphosed woman in history or literature for them to go by. Apparently the female arriviste has to be either of the Marilyn Monroe-Holly Golightly type, whose means of self-advancement are obvious; or of the bohemian-artistic type; or the earnest drudge.

When I, who fit into none of these categories but could pass unnoticed in a convention of Rotary Anns, tell people I was born a hillbilly, they are likely to ask merrily, "You mean you wore a calico dress and went running barefooted through the hills?" When I say yes, it doesn't register. But I really did. I wore a calico dress *and* a calico bonnet, and I ran around barefooted over hills and fields about two thirds of every year till I was thirteen. My parents and my grandparents, not to mention their forebears on both sides for eight or ten generations, were born in log cabins, as I was, and we all spoke the Appalachian mountain dailect. Their most remote American ancestors came from the mountains along the Scotch-English border in the seventeenth century and settled in the mountains of North Carolina. From there, some of them drifted into the Kentucky and Tennessee Appalachians, which is where all my great grandparents came from (by ox-drawn wagons) to the Missouri Ozarks in the 1840s. They brought their culture with them and held on to it, and I spent my childhood surrounded by it.

But I have given up trying to make people believe that. Even if they accept it as the truth that I spent my childhood in the Ozarks, they prefer to believe that it was by some accident—such as that my father, an eccentric professor or some such, was studying the effect of folk culture on intellectual development and was using me as a case study.

To conceive of a totally assimilated female as having had unmitigatedly low-class, rustic origins requires an effort of the imagination, even in this democracy, that I find it uncharitable to call upon my acquaintances to make. At a social gathering a few years ago, and before I had learned about this difficulty, I found myself in conversation with the father of another of my high-school classmates who had been misled by my protective coloration. This child had struck up a rapport with me in biology class, and after class one day she told me she was going to propose me for membership in her social sorority. By then, as I knew, many of her sorority sisters were aware of my anomalous social position, but Elizabeth Anne was new in town, besides being exceptionally naïve. Chiefly to save her the embarrassment of backing a certain loser, I gently but firmly declined the honor, though I knew I couldn't explain why without implying that I regarded her and her friends as snobs. Instead, I left her feeling rejected and hurt.

Years later, when I was telling her father about the episode, it all seemed to me rather funny and touching, and I couldn't see that it reflected unfavorably on either of the children involved—his daughter or myself. At any rate, it seemed quite unconnected with my adult self, so I was surprised when the man reacted as if I had committed a severe breach of the proprieties. He stared at me a moment as if shocked to speechlessness, then turned and walked away. I surmised then that he was offended with me for having deceived him by carrying on with my social charade, but perhaps he was suffering retroactively with those two well-meaning children.

If I had no expectations of elevating myself socially by going to high school, neither did I regard it as the sole means by which I could develop my intelligence. My father looked on formal schooling as mere regimentation, and believed that the only real education was self-education. I suspected he was right, and any doubts I might have had on the point were offset by his example. He had gone to school for only a few months, when some itinerant schoolmaster had set up shop in Polk County one year, but he wrote a fine Spencerian hand, and had learned algebra (even if he did call it "algebry"), geometry, and Latin by himself, and I considered him as wise and learned a man as I ever expected to meet.

The only real attraction school had for me lay in its being the one place where I could excel. At home, I had been considered slow and lazy, and it was true that housework and farm chores were so uncongenial to me that I shirked them, even when I knew I was letting myself in for a switching by my stepmother. And my proficiency at book-learning, far from mitigating my reputation for sloth, had been taken as certain evidence of it. I had always avoided referring to my scholastic triumphs at home, and none of the other eligible children in our ménage had elected to attend while I was in the one-room country schools where they would have found me out. But if a neighbor child happened to drop a remark about how smart Ethel was in school, my stepmother would seize the occasion to carry on at length about how any idiot could be smart in school if all they did was to keep their nose in a book and pester other people with questions about things that were none of their business. I could see that she was right, and that my peculiar propensities were in the nature of handicaps, except when I *was* in school.

I really looked on going to school, therefore, as an end in itself, and to achieve it, I was willing to forgo temporarily the pleasures of friendship and family affection. If I could have foreseen, as my father seemed to, that I was taking on a lifetime membership in what we both regarded as the pretentious, dreary middle class by adapting to its norms in high school, I might have stayed in the hills with the rest of the family and continued to talk Ozark for the rest of my days. But I didn't know then that my adaptation had to be permanent.

2

FOR THOU ART WITH ME

My father's early favoritism for me was a natural outcome of his having been my only parent from the time I was two until he married again when I was five. My mother —his second wife—died in childbirth shortly after my second birthday. Both of my parents then had adolescent daughters by previous marriages, and the big girls took care of me after my mother's death. But my father was my world.

In my first vivid memory of him, I was four years old and our family was moving, in a train of three or four wagons, from the place where I was born, which had belonged to my mother, to a house four or five miles away, which my father had rented. It was a bitterly cold day, though we children were snug in a covered wagon, which was heated with an oil stove, where we were being cared for by some of the neighbor women. But I was miserable because I didn't know where my father was. I finally started bawling so inconsolably that the ladies had the drivers stop the wagons, and one of them led me up to the first one, which my father was driving, using our ice-cold kitchen stove for a seat. They hoisted me up beside him, he gave me a comforting pat on my black-stockinged knee, and I sat there in frozen bliss all the rest of the way to our new abode.

Soon after we got to the new house, my oldest half-sister, Grace—a young grass widow who was the mother of the three other small children in our ménage—got together a quick meal and served it on some new granite plates that my father had ordered from Monkey Ward's to replace my mother's dishes. The meager furniture was still not arranged, so we little kids were standing up to eat. I found myself at a corner of the table, untempted by the food on the strange white enameled plate in front of me, and I just stood there, feeling miserable and unable to function.

Eventually Blanche, my ten-year-old half-sister, noticed my pitiful state. "Look at Ethel," she said. "She ain't eat a bite."

"I know what's the matter," Grace said. "She has to set by Papa."

I didn't know that that was what was ailing me, but their continued impatient urgings failed to move me, and finally Grace got up and found my high stool and put it up at the other end of the table by my father. He hoisted me up, put the same plate in front of me, and suddenly the food on it looked delicious.

Actually my father had an unbounded love for all children, and his idea of the good life was to be surrounded by them, his own or other people's, and to be able to supply just enough food and sufficient shelter to keep them healthy. He was happy to work hard all day for the reward of having us run out to greet him eagerly when he came in in the evening, as we always did. The ritual then was for him to chuckle affectionately, swing the youngest one up over his head and carry him into the house, on his shoulder, with the rest of us tagging at his heels.

Even though the house on my mother's farm—an inheritance from her first husband—was built of logs, the land around it was ample and productive enough that my father had been able to support us all, including her four children, his four, his three grandchildren and me, by farming it. Our new place had a smaller log house and very little acreage, and, for the year we lived there, my father had to work away from home at carpentry, his only trade, or as a farm hand. We had had to move from the first farm because my mother's parents, who were solid fundamental Baptists, had gone to court and gotten custody of her four children and control of the farm on the grounds that my father was not a fit parent. The evidence he produced that he was kind to the children, worked hard to provide for them, and was of good moral character counted as nothing alongside the testimony of my grandparents that he was a Socialist and an agnostic and didn't make the children go to Sunday school. Like most of the rest of his fellow Polk Countians, the judge was a Republican and a Baptist, and if my father's religious and political nonconformism hadn't disqualified him as a parent in the judge's eyes, his unconcern for worldly goods would have cinched it. His net worth, after the forced sale of his and my mother's community property, was about five hundred dollars.

Actually, my father would always have been more affluent if he himself had not been so thoroughly imbued with Christian tenets. Though he acknowledged no belief in a supernatural power, he still lived according to his parents' teachings, founded on the notion that if you were hard-working, honest, thrifty, kind, and generous, the Lord would provide. I grew up detesting the bigoted judge who had taken my mother's other children away from my father—it was losing them that he most lamented —though I no longer remembered them. So far did I diverge from my father's teachings, however, that a dozen years later, when fate had thrown me into a rather intimate relationship with that judge, I regarded him only as an absurd little man, not worth the trouble it would have taken to oversalt his soup. He was small, tidy, hen-pecked, and finicking; slept in a nightshirt; read only the comics and the sports pages of the newspapers; and was old and afraid of dying. I served his soup and ironed his nightshirts with no feeling toward him whatever—except, perhaps, a little scornful amusement. I was in my first term of college—young, healthy, free, with my life ahead of me. My father would never have understood how I could have acted in the capacity of a servant to his old enemy and still have felt superior to him, so I never mentioned the judge in my letters back to Newton County.

By that time I had discovered that my father's truths were relative. I knew that he would never consciously misrepresent anything whatever, but I had also learned that, about the big truths, his view was distorted by a naïve faith in the triumph of good over evil. Even his avowed atheism seemed to me to be the result of a too optimistic view of reality. Until I was in my mid-teens, I strongly suspected that there *was* a Hell and that he and I both would end up there—I from choosing to cast my lot with him. I had sensed at a tender age that his true attitude toward Old Jehovey, as he referred to God, was not disbelief but dislike. He professed not to believe the Bible, yet he used it to find evidence of the folly, cruelty, small-mindedness, and vindictiveness of his unequal adversary, particularly when he ran short of items from the daily events that struck him as evidence of the same divine flaws. The most heinous of these to him were disasters involving children; these used to send him into Job-like lamentations.

The idea of God that I got from the revivalist meetings that were my early contact with organized religion was very close to the one that my father, by indirection, had lodged in my head, and it seemed to me that His nonexistence was too much to hope for. It never occurred to my father that his own running feud with the Almighty had imbued all his children with a vivid belief in some sort of omnipotent tyrant in the sky, and he was thwarted and baffled, in his declining years, by the knowledge that all of them but me had seen the wisdom of aligning themselves with superior strength, and that even I had given up the battle. Once when I was grown I asked him why he got so mad at God if he didn't believe He existed. He looked startled for a moment, and then said ruefully, "For *not* existing, I guess."

When I was ten and we were living temporarily in a Joplin slum of mine and smelter workers, I had barely escaped being saved once at a revival meeting. We children and my stepmother had started going to church there, in the summer as an alternative to the free silent movies at Schifferdecker Park when we had already seen the feature, and in the fall and winter after the park had closed.

Various kinds of Fundamentalist preachers, all known to us as Holy Rollers, came and went in the role of masters of ceremonies at the church, but the other star performers were regulars. They were the more extroverted members of the congregation who were adept at "testifying" and speaking in tongues, and who sometimes actually did roll in the floor. I found the tales they told in their testifyings even more gripping than those in the true-confession magazines I had taken to reading, but somehow all of us in the audience seemed to have reached a tacit agreement that the secrets divulged in these rituals were not to be gossiped about outside. It was not only that the final redemption of the testifiers was felt to have wiped out the guilt of their former selves but also that we took it for granted that one was permitted a certain amount of poetic license in a church, whether from the floor or the pulpit.

Periodically one of the roving preachers would conduct a revival or "protracted meeting"—which my father always liked to call "distracted meetings"—and then we more dedicated churchgoers went every night. One night, I was carried away by a luridly graphic demonstration, in colored chalk on a portable chalkboard, of the prophecies of Revelation by an evangelist who drew lines, as in a school for butchers, on some kind of fantastic beast. I never did get the point of the demonstration but the main point sank home. A loving Jesus was waiting to enter my heart and save me from certain undefined red, orange, and purple horrors. By the time the call came for candidates at the mourners' bench, I was sure that I was one of those who had obeyed the preacher's command to open my heart and let Him in. The conviction lasted until it came my turn to complete the transaction under the guidance of the preacher and a couple of his acolytes, and then it deserted me. The fervent prayers of all the congregation failed to restore it, so I returned to my seat with mingled feelings of having let everybody and God down rather horribly, and of being a reject, which feelings were balanced by a glow of self-righteousness at my honesty under great temptation (which I thought God, at least, would appreciate), and relief at having had a narrow escape.

A certain coolness developed between me and some of the leading members of the congregation after that and I felt that this was exacerbated at Christmastime. For those services the ladies' aid had provided a Christmas tree under which they stacked small sacks of cheap candy for the "poor children." My father was out of work that season, and we weren't expecting any candy in our stockings, but I remained conspicuously in my seat and was not even tempted when we were invited to come and accept the gifts. The prospect of leaving the nice ladies with a surplus of their bounty that they would have to eat themselves appealed to me more than the candy, and I forcibly restrained my stepbrother George, whose appetite outweighed his pride, from parading up for his share. After that I never did attend church regularly again except for the one term I went to a Baptist college.

But I was fifteen and in high school before I dared to allow myself the liberty of exploring my own religious doubts to their limits, without fear that the all-seeing Thought Monitor up there was just waiting for me to reach the point of ultimate disbelief before retaliating. My liberation was the result of issuing a challenge to God —in the presence of a theretofore believing witness—to strike me dead. I didn't know then how trite that performance was or that the record indicates that the Deity always spurns a show of strength as a response to that particular challenge. If I had, I could have spared myself a moment of near heart-stopping suspense.

In any case, the experiment demonstrated to my satisfaction that either Old Jehovey was no longer in control
or, at least, that you could doubt with impunity. Also
adding to my intellectual liberation were the intimations
of pantheism that I was picking up from the poets and
novelists. *Thanatopsis* struck me as rather *avant-garde,*
and I feared that William Ernest Henley had robbed me
of earthly immortality by having said so perfectly in *In-
victus* what I would have said if he hadn't beaten me to it.

So far as I knew, the girl who acted as a witness to my
experiment was the only one of my classmates who had
any religious doubts, and I was mostly responsible for
those. I was therefore thrilled and amazed at the temerity
of our chemistry teacher, who discussed non-Biblical theories of creation and so forth, without trying to make
them jibe with the Bible, and I was equally amazed at the
equanimity with which my fellow students received his
heretical notions. In fact, I scrupulously refrained from
asking the provocative questions I sometimes wanted to
ask, and from pointing out the extent of the teacher's
heresy, from a feeling that I was in a conspiracy with the
teacher to permit the truth to be spread insidiously, and
without my tempting him to jeopardize his job.

For my first semester of college, I went back to Bolivar,
in the county I was born in, to live with my maternal
grandmother and a spinster aunt and attend a Baptist
junior college there. My relatives offered me the use of a
bedroom, and I arranged to earn my board, and money
for incidental expenses by doing the housework for the
judge, whose wife was a semi-invalid. At that college, of
all places, I encountered another free-thinking teacher,
and with that one I entered into an acknowledged conspiracy.

This one was the French teacher—a small, wiry, red-bearded Swede, who spoke British English with a trace of a German accent. He had taught English in Spain and Russian in Germany and was then translating the Bible from Greek into Hungarian. He got the notion that I was a fellow rebel one day when he was practicing French on the class by discussing the news, and asked us which candidate we were for in the presidential election. I was sitting in the front row, and I looked around to see how my classmates voted as Professor Nelson called the candidates' names. I really had no political attachments then, and I didn't hold up my hand for the Republican, or the Democrat, or the Socialist, all of whom, including even the last, had too many adherents in the class to interest me in indicating an affiliation. Then I saw that the professor was watching me, and when he called the Communist candidate's name, I held up my hand out of daredeviltry.

I don't think any of my classmates noticed, or if they did that they considered it significant, but Professor Nelson stopped me after class and said he had to talk to me. He took me into his little office across the hall and, instead of censuring me, as I had expected, unburdened himself of all the thoughts on politics and fundamental religion he had kept bottled up for the couple of years he had been in that uncongenial atmosphere. He soon learned that I was quite ignorant, if receptive, politically, but he thought I was more advanced philosophically than he was. He had lost his religion, too, but he regretted it, whereas I professed to consider it an accomplishment.

Professor Nelson had an un-American smile: it was wide, ingenuous and unself-conscious, and all the more disconcerting because his teeth, though square, strong, and well-formed, were a glossy black. When I answered his questions about my religious beliefs, with a flippancy that he seemed to find deliciously shocking, he would smile that slow, childlike smile at me and exclaim at my precociousness.

"Ah! And so *young!*" he would say beamishly. "I was afraid to say even to *myself* that I doubted until I was thirty. How could you be so brave!"

He talked to me that first day through the next hour, which we both had free, and through half of his next class, which he had forgotten about, and suddenly remembered in a great flurry of collecting books and papers, amid groans and smiles, and apologies for keeping me so long.

Besides sharing an interest in philosophy and metaphysics, the professor and I also discovered a common fascination with etymology. One day he told the class about the phenomenon of "folk etymology," and how it had affected French and English interchanges: how "ouragan" and "dent-de-lion" had become "hurricane" and "dandelion" by the same process that, on the other side of the Channel, produced "redingote" and "canif" from "riding coat" and "knife." He also told us about the common origin of the Indo-European languages: how all of the dozen languages he had studied, except Chinese and Hungarian, had grown from one prehistoric tongue. This struck me then (and still does) as one of the most marvelous things I'd heard in all my life. But the rest of the students were unimpressed, and, since I was learning then to conceal my intellectual curiosity, I waited until after class to pursue the topic further.

The professor lent me some books on linguistics, along with some of the works of his fellow freethinkers—Shaw, Russell, and Mencken—and, altogether, we had so many fascinating things to talk about, and talked about them so secretively—breaking off when anybody else came within earshot—that we began to create suspicions. Professor Nelson looked so odd, dressed so queerly, and seemed to me so old (he was in his late fifties) that I brushed off the wisecracks of my fellow students. I guessed that they were more just curious than actually suspicious of any sexual attraction between the professor and me. But he also began to route his daily five-mile constitutional by my grandmother's house, and she and my aunt developed an interest in our relationship that caused me more concern. They lived in a big old house that was next to the last one on the main street of the small country town, and I would see the professor come plodding down the street, in a gait that I imagined he had picked up in imitation of the peasants in Hungary, and I would stroll out to meet him. Then we would talk so long and so animatedly, he with wild gestures and exclamations and uninhibited laughter, that my two sedate Baptist relatives, watching from behind the curtains, were scandalized without knowing just why. They had little doubt that the odd, exuberant foreigner had improper designs upon me, and, though I was certain that his interest in me was purely platonic, I still felt almost as guilty as if I had been flirting with him. I knew, anyway, that if my relatives had known what we *were* talking about, they would have found it no less scandalous than sex, so I eventually yielded to their disapproval and stopped seeing the professor on his evening marches down the highway, though we kept up our on-campus discussions, to the disgust and bemusement of my younger, less exotic friends.

Professor Nelson's awe at my intellectual daring at so tender an age paled beside that I felt at his cold-blooded hypocrisy. I dutifully went to chapel every day and to church on Sunday, but I sat in the back, looked straight ahead during prayers, and resolutely kept silent during hymns addressed to the Lord. After I had heard the professor's avowal of outright atheism, I marveled to see him sitting and amen-ing with the elders that Sunday and, when he was asked the next Sunday to lead the congregation in prayer, I was horrified. I watched in thrilled trepidation as he intoned the familiar pious phrases, and it would not have surprised me at all if he had been felled with a thunderbolt. In fact, I was greatly surprised that he was not. It was one thing to challenge the Deity on the steps of the Carnegie Library, as I had done, and quite another to mock Him in a church.

I knew that my professor wasn't really a very good teacher, at least for freshman American students of French; the apathy and ineptness of the other members of my class soon caused him to abandon any serious attempt to help them learn the language. I also knew, because he told me so, that he had lost other jobs because of his nonconformism. Still, I couldn't really forgive him for faking religiousness, even to eat, and our relationship cooled after I had watched a couple of his performances in church.

It was a relief to learn a couple of years later that Professor Nelson and the Baptists had parted company, and that he had gone to Mexico to teach Italian to some Catholics.

As for me, Russell, Mencken, and Shaw became my God-cum-father substitutes and remained that till they all got married, or remarried, and disillusioned me.

Epilogue

Years later, after I had read Mencken's books on American speech, it happened that I wrote to him about some misconceptions he had expressed concerning the way Ozarkers talk and why, and how so-called General American really strikes their ears and why. He was most interested in my analysis and urged me to write about it for publication. He said that he didn't know of any other student of dialects who had actually spoken an illiterate one as his native tongue. He added, "An account of the reaction of such a person to formal language should be fascinating. I don't think it has ever been done."

My first published pieces, outside of those done for local newspapers, were the result of trying to act on that suggestion, as is this book, in part. Thus did Professor Nelson, the epitome of the ridiculous and inept teacher, indirectly affect the course of my life.

Teachers beware.

3

CULTURE IN THE HILLS

There are hillbillies and hillbillies, of course.

Polk County, to which I had returned for my first semester of college, is on a fertile Ozarks plateau and was
connected, long before I was born, by a good surfaced
road and by the Frisco railroad, to Springfield, which
Mencken once described as the "Paris and Gomorrah of
the Ozarks." The cultural tone in that area is therefore
somewhat more civilized than that in Newton and Mc-
Donald counties, which are in the less arable hills along
the Arkansas border.

The only batch of totally uncivilized hillbillies I had
ever seen before we left Polk County were the Sweeneys,
who lived somewhere up the road from us. And the only
times I saw them were when they would straggle by our
house in a group, everybody, including the adults, barefooted, the men unshaven, and the patriarch riding on a
jinny, which was accoutered fore and aft with cooking
utensils and the like. We had no idea where the Sweeneys
went, but the supposition was that they were going to
visit some other Sweeneys. We used to run out and watch
their exodus, like a parade, and, two or three days later,

their return. One of us would yell, "Here come the Sweeneys!" (I thought the word was a common noun, like "gypsy") and we would run out to the rail fence in front of our house and watch them meander by, they utterly indifferent to our interest in them.

Then there were the Wares. Grandpa and Grannie Ware were anachronisms. Born of the first generation of pioneers who settled the region in the 1840s, they lived, in the second decade of the twentieth century, exactly as their parents did. Grannie Ware had a dried-apple face and smoked a clay pipe and always wore dark, full-skirted dresses that came below her shoe-tops and, when out of doors, a bonnet to match. She was lithe, agile, and endlessly busy. She had a spinning wheel and a loom and could convert raw wool, which she herself sheared from sheep she had raised herself, into coverlids, stockings, and linsey-woolsey. She made her own dyes, favoring walnut stain, and knew how to make all the old remedies from herbs. Grandpa Ware, though he must not have been much older than Grannie, had quit working by the time I knew him. He used to sit in a rocking chair on their front porch all day, his features obscured by his unbarbered, snow-white hair and beard, and whittle.

The Ware brood consisted of four strapping and handsome sons, and a daughter, Corey, who was an imbecile and crippled. It was said that Corey had been a beautiful, healthy baby—that Grannie had a photograph to prove it—until she had suffered an attack of brain fever that caused her head to swell until her skull split when she was four. Their good looks notwithstanding, the Ware boys were generally considered a little too untamed to make good husband material for girls of the better sort in the neighborhood, and they all married late, and badly, except Charlie, the oldest.

Charlie, our nearest Ware neighbor, had been thoroughly tamed by an early marriage and himself had a brood of nubile sons and daughters. He was one of my father's converts to Socialism, and his oldest son, Hiram, was courting my oldest unmarried half-sister, Fragile.

The leading Socialist in their group was Frank Lloyd, who was rich and educated. He contributed the money and my father the plans and supervisory skill to build a Socialist hall in the neighborhood. There the men had their political meetings and the young people had social affairs and cultural gatherings—square dances, tacky parties, singin's, "dialogues" (as they called plays), and debates.

Fragile was taking organ lessons and had learned to play "Down by the Old Mill Stream," "When You Wore a Tulip," "There's a Long, Long Trail a-Winding," and "Tipperary." Ed Ware, the most rambunctious of the Ware boys, had gotten into trouble with the law—I think by setting himself up a still, out behind the Ware orchard —and was on the lam for a while. He sneaked in from his hideout one night and regaled his brothers with a tale of having sat high up in a tree while the sheriff, whose name was Esau Blue, and his bloodhounds had passed below. Ed boasted that he had thrown the dogs off the scent by putting red pepper in his socks.

Fragile's group, inspired by the sheriff's name, worked Ed's tale into a parody of one of the popular songs and sang it in harmony, gathered around the organ, always bearing down strongly on the line, "That's where 'e saw Blue, and his bloodhounds too." For years I thought those

were the only words for that barbershop favorite, and
that tricking a pursuing lawman was an amusing thing
to do.

That frivolous life was to end soon. There was talk of
war. Fragile and Hiram got married. And Papa was misled by a couple of Kansas City Socialists into putting his
five hundred dollars into a communal fund and moving
us all to Newton County and the Ozark Cooperative
Home Colony.

Our family and the Charlie Wares joined up together.
We all went by train to Neosho, where we were met by a
representative of the Kansas City men—two brothers
named Hartley—and were taken to the farm where the
colony was to be set up.

We were among the first arrivals, who were also the
last. Papa was to increase his apiary and be in charge of
building the houses. Others were assigned other tasks.
There was a large orchard on the place, and there were
plans to raise chickens and hogs and produce the food
for them and for the colonists. (The Hartley brothers had
mills in Kansas City and were to do the grain processing.)

There was one large house on the place in which three
families were to live temporarily, one of them consisting
of Fragile and Hiram, who were expecting a child. There
was also one large storehouse on a high foundation with
wooden steps leading up to the front door, which looked
like a general store and was to serve as a store—community owned.

The rest of us moved into tents. My father built a floor
and some low sidewalls for ours and for the one Grace
and her family lived in, and it was a good thing he did.
We moved in in the spring and there were still no permanent dwellings built when winter started.

By then, things had pretty well fallen apart; the money in the community fund was gone and the men had started working for hire, on other farms and in Neosho, to support their families. We and two other families then moved into the storehouse, which was divided lengthwise into four parts by curtains, three parts used for sleeping quarters and one for a community kitchen and sitting room.

By that time, our family had been increased by three. When we first got settled in our tent, my father, full of utopian dreams, went back to Polk County and married Louie Ware's widow, Agnes. Louie had been killed instantly the year before when a mule kicked him in the head, and had left a widow and two small children. The widow, now my stepmother, was somewhat younger than my half-sister Grace. She was very fat, had a pretty, childlike face, and she called my father Mr. Reed.

Agnes was spoiled and had a short temper and there was some discord in the longhouse. Still, I found life in the colony interesting and pleasant. I was not to be six until December, but I started to school that fall and there found my métier. My little stepsister had her mother's pretty face, and my little stepbrother was good-natured, and I loved them both. My stepmother didn't understand me and was jealous of me besides, but it was easy to keep out of her way most of the time.

I soon learned that what annoyed her most about me was my incessant questions about everything, including a good many she had never given a thought to. The others in the family had come to regard the habit as a kind of tic which it was usually better to ignore. But my stepmother half-suspected that I was persecuting her, and it must have seemed that way at first when I still consid-

ered her as a possible new source of information and was
asking her things the others hadn't known, such as what
"reg us pat off" meant, and how cows knew where to dig
when they went to find their calves.

She soon diagnosed my trouble as idiocy complicated
by sexual obsessions. The way she put it was that I was
touched in the head and had a dirty mind. I thought she
was probably right, but the possibility that I was an idiot
didn't disturb me very much, except that I wondered if I
would have to wear tennis shoes all my life. I had seen
the town nut on the main street of Neosho and had observed that he seemed to wear that kind of footgear the
year round. Still, he always looked happier than the other
people on the streets and he was treated with kindness
and respect. Having a dirty mind was clearly a more unattractive handicap but one that I felt equally powerless
to rid myself of. My trouble was that I hadn't yet learned
anything about sex and therefore didn't yet know which
questions to avoid. Not long after my stepmother came,
however, there were three enlightening developments,
all involving her newly acquired Newton County Ware
in-laws who lived across the road. She didn't know about
the first episode, luckily for me. It concerned a couple of
dates I had noticed on the flyleaf of the family Bible
which she had brought with her from Polk County and
which my father had filled in for her. One morning when
I was visiting Ed Ware's new wife, she was talking with
her sister, who had also walked up the road to visit, about
multiple births and other such anomalies of childbearing,
and it occurred to me that I had an interesting item to
contribute.

"Agnes had a baby thirteen days after her and Louie
Ware got married," I said.

I was puzzled and alarmed by the effect of my conversational contribution. The two women exchanged knowing smirks, and Aunt Almy said, "Did you hear that, Etta? I thought it was funny a feller like Louie would marry *her*, if he was all they say. How do you know, Ethel? Did she tell you, or are you just makin' it up?"

I said, "I saw it in the Bible. It says, 'Agnes Jones—married—Louie Ware—January 1, 1913. Ware infant—born dead—January 14, 1913.'" Again the women looked at each other knowingly, and Aunt Etta decided to test my reading ability by trying me out on the kitchen calendar. I had sensed by then that what I had said reflected in some way on my stepmother and I regretted saying it, but I passed the reading test easily. I had learned the numbers from a similar calendar in our own kitchen, and I could even read the hard words on it—"Cardui," "Black Draught" (which I called "black drawt"), and "women's complaints." Aunt Almy advised me not to tell anyone at home that I had told them about the interesting dates, but I had already decided that it would be best not to.

Not long after that I was visiting with my stepmother at Aunt Etta's house down the road—the last time, she said later, that she would ever take me anywhere—when Aunt Etta remarked that she was going to have to shut her cow up in the barn that night because she was due to find a calf. I had thought it was especially marvelous that such large things as calves and colts could lie around waiting for their mothers to find them without ever being visible to people, and I had been told that this was because animals dug their young out of the ground. Then of course I wondered why farmers didn't occasionally turn up a baby animal when they were plowing, how the mothers knew exactly where to dig, and how they acted when they had finally reached pay dirt. That a cow could unearth her destined treasure when restricted to the small area of the floor of her stall seemed to me to be marvelous almost beyond belief, and the opportunity of watching her at her soundings easily worth losing a night's sleep.

I asked my stepmother eagerly if I could come back and spend the night in the barn watching, and she looked aghast. "I won't be sleepy, honest," I promised. "And I'll set up in the manger, out of the way."

Embarrassedly trying to ignore me, she made some hasty parting remarks to Aunt Etta, and yanked me out the door. When we got out of sight up the road, she swatted me on the behind several times, and told me that no decent-minded kid would have any interest in watching such a sight, reminded me that I was not only an idiot but an evil-minded idiot, and told me never to ask to go anywhere with her again.

I had already learned that grownups were capable of lying to children about certain things—the year before that, back in Polk County, when I was four, I had learned about Santa Claus. On Christmas Eve, we had each hung a stocking on a broomstick, suspended on the backs of two chairs, and when we little kids came downstairs on Christmas morning, there were large snowy footprints leading from the front door to the stockings and back. The big kids seemed to me to be just a little over-eager for us to notice the footprints, and I got suspicious. When no one was looking, I opened the closet door to see if my father's overshoes had fresh snow on them. They did. I kept the knowledge to myself, and I don't know now whether my reticence was due to a regrettable streak of slyness or to a wish not to disappoint the older children who were trying so hard.

From testing him out on the Santa Claus issue, I had learned that my father would not lie but also that he was good at avoiding straight answers. The next Sunday after I had disgraced myself at Aunt Etta's, I went out to the apiary, where he was working on his bees and asked him if it was true that cows dug up their calves. He said, "Some people say that."

I said, "And do doctors really bring babies to their mothers in their doctor satchels?"

He went on working and said without looking at me, "Oh, I reckon that's one way of puttin' it. It'll do for now."

I saw then that I was going to have to find out about babies on my own, and it wasn't long before I got a good clue, back at Aunt Almy's house. This time I was spending the day with her by request. Uncle Ed was away, and I was told that Aunt Almy might suddenly need a doctor. If she took sick, I was to run as fast as I could and let Aunt Etta know.

I was watching Aunt Almy as she swept the front room, and I decided that she looked very healthy to be expecting to get sick. All I could see wrong with her was that she had developed an alarming bulge in her belly. Adding things up, I arrived at what seemed to me a fantastic conclusion, and I suddenly asked her point-blank if she was going to have a baby.

"Now what makes you think a thing like that?" she asked, feigning shock.

My boldness ebbed. "That," I said bashfully, pointing at her belly.

"You mean this?" she said, displaying a large pocket on her apron. "You think I'm going to carry a baby in this?"

I gave up, but I resolved to watch and see if Aunt Almy did have a baby, and if so, whether the bulge in her belly went down. Within a week I had the answers to that phase of the baby question.

I was comparatively retarded about discovering sex, however. I had wanted to be a boy ever since I could first remember, and after somebody told me that a girl could change herself into a boy by kissing her elbow, I tried hard to do that, finally making a mental note to take advantage of the occasion if I should ever be lucky enough to break my arm. But I'm sure that my precocious preference for the masculine role had nothing to do with penis envy, as the child psychologists so crudely call it. I had already been trying to kiss my elbow for several months before I learned that boy children were physically different from girl children in any other way than their style of haircuts. Then I was watching Grace make a pair of underpants for her son, Carl, one day, and asked her why she was making an opening in the front of them. She told me that boys had a little thing on them they used through the opening when they had to "go out." I could see no special advantage to that, but learning that there was a difference reminded me that Carl had once offered to show me what he had in exchange for a look at mine and that I hadn't wanted to play. I told Grace about it. She assured me, mildly, that I had done the right thing and told me never to play any games like that that boys might ask me to play.

The impression this conversation made on me led a while later to my first (and last, I believe) bit of gold-digging. The opportunity arose after we moved to the colony, where there were several boys who were a couple of years older than my half-niece, Jessie, and I. One fall evening, about dusk, Jessie and I and some other pre-schoolers wandered out to where some of the boys had

built a bonfire and were roasting some potatoes. They had
filched butter, salt, and pepper and were enjoying a de-
licious-looking feast. It was suppertime and they knew
we were hungry, and, after ignoring us for a while, they
had a huddle and decided to make us a proposition: they
would give us each a roasted, seasoned potato if we would
look at their sexual organs. We were reluctant but finally
agreed, on condition that they gave us the potatoes first.
We ate our potatoes, then the boys formed a trusting little
circle in the light of the bonfire. The other little girls took
their punishment, one by one, each rejoining our doomed
little group with the disillusioned air of having been
roundly gypped. Finally it was my turn, but I shut my
eyes tight and refused to look, even after one of the larger
boys had pulled me into the circle and ordered me to do
so. I knew I had cheated, however, and I felt so guilty
about it that I never after that let myself become ob-
ligated to any member of that sex who might expect an
analogous favor in return.

By the next spring it became obvious to everyone that
the Ozark Cooperative Home Colony was a failure, so my
father got a job with a contractor in Neosho and moved
us to a rented house a few miles away. This house, which
was situated on the highway to Joplin, was built of horizontal planks painted red and looked disconcertingly like
a barn.

What I liked best about living at the Red House was
what we used for a Sunday recreation area there. Sunday
was always a special day, even in our nonreligious house.
Saturday was house-cleaning and baking day, and Saturday night we all took turns bathing in a washtub in the
middle of the kitchen floor. On Sunday mornings we all
put on clean clothes, and my father dyed his mustache

and shaved. During the winter, my father would repair our shoes for the rest of the mornings—he had lasts in three or four sizes for half-soling and an awl for repairing stitches—and would spend the afternoons reading. From the spring through the fall, Papa would tend his bees in the morning and would take us all on a picnic in the afternoon, if the weather was fair.

If we lived where a branch or a creek was within walking distance, we would go there on Sunday afternoons, taking a picnic lunch in a basket. My father would find a place to fish, while we children, stripped down to our underpants, waded and dogpaddled in the shallower water, or, according to the season, picked flowers or hunted hazelnuts, pawpaws, and persimmons. There was no stream near the Red House, so we picnicked that summer at what my father called "the old house place," a quiet, grassy glade, deep in the woods behind our house and a mile or so away. It was marked by the remains of an old stone chimney and well house and by luxuriant growths of once domesticated flowers and plants—roses, irises, lilac bushes, asparagus, rhubarb—that must have been flourishing on their own for ages. (The old house place, too, recurs in my dreams, bathed in a haunting, magic light. In my dreams I am always there alone, alerted by the portentous *ambiance* of the place to expect something marvelous to happen. But nothing ever does, and I awake feeling haunted and bereft.)

I didn't enter the school in the new district until fall, but the very first day the teacher promoted me to the second grade, and when I got home that afternoon I got another lesson in cynicism. The path to the school was through the woods behind our house, so when I got home the first person I saw was my father, who was chopping wood. I started running, and when I got within earshot I yelled, "Papa! Papa! Guess what grade I'm in!"

"Oh, the second I guess," he said, and went on with his chopping.

I stood stunned at his omniscience for a moment. Then I saw the logic of his deduction and accepted it resignedly. I didn't bother to tell anyone else.

By that time the Ware tribe had resettled in all around us. Grannie found, slap on top of a steep hill, a place that might have been designed with her in mind. It was a weathered log house with some equally weathered outbuildings, with just enough level ground spreading back from the road for a garden, a chicken yard, a hog lot, and pasture for a few sheep, a cow, and a team of horses. Grannie was soon buzzing about gathering herbs, weeding tomatoes, and doing all the other chores inside and outside the house. Grandpa Ware had taken up his spot on the front porch.

By then, I was related to Grannie twice by marriage, in a typical Ozarks relationship. She was the grandmother of my stepsister and brother and the great grandmother of my half-niece. The Ozarkers didn't marry cousins, but by the time of my birth everybody in Polk County was related to me and to everybody else there through intermarriage of more remote connections.

My quasi-granddaughterly relationship with Grannie Ware bestowed on me the privilege of occasional weekend visits, my real grandmothers still being back in Polk County. I looked forward to the visits as not only a welcome change of scene but a vacation from onerous chores. At home, even at five and six, I had such boring chores as having to watch the little kids and keep them amused, having to pick up chips for kindling every morning and evening, and having to pull grass for the penned-up chickens. (I still remember that last chore as the most irksome one I ever had to do, probably because I once got a switching for cheating at it. Ordered to fill a bucket with grass before I stopped to play, I got it about half full and then buried a big rock under the grass. I expected to be found out and punished, but almost any kind of punishment I could imagine struck me at the time as the lesser of two evils. The smell of bruised grass still makes me feel a little tired to this day.)

Grannie preferred to do her own chores, requiring of young visitors only that they keep out of her way. She seemed to utilize everything that grew on her small patch of land, including the weeds and briers. I have a clear memory of her flitting around among the dead weeds and brier patches picking off small bunches of wool, which her sheep had lost in transit, to save for carding and spinning, though that seems unlikely.

It never occurred to me to wonder why Grannie wanted us children to visit her. It was taken for granted among the hillbillies that a child of any kind was an asset to any household, but I've always supposed that that was because they added to the work force or could be enjoyed for their companionship. To Grannie, however, we contributed nothing but more chores, and now it occurs to me that she might have wanted us as playmates for Aunt Corey. Aunt Corey could churn and dry dishes but otherwise she was idle and bored when there were no children around, and Grannie must have been more concerned about her than she seemed to be.

Aunt Corey was a disconcerting playmate for a small child. She could play club fist and other hand games—not well but with a delight that made up for her ineptitude—

but she used two canes to get around with, and stand-up games had to be modified for her. She could speak only a few words, and those not very intelligibly, but that was not a serious handicap to someone used to having to entertain infants. What spoiled Aunt Corey's favorite game of tag for me was that she liked to play it using one of her canes, and she would sometimes start a game without warning. A sharp crack on the skull would be the first signal that a new game was on. I would yelp in pained surprise, and Aunt Corey would be delighted.

What I most enjoyed at Grannie's house was wandering to the foot of the hill and watching the hydraulic ram in the branch there. It throbbed incessantly, with a metallically liquid, rhythmic clink, like the heart of Grannie's mountain, somehow forcing water up the hill to the house. I can't imagine how it ever got there or how we happened to know the technical name for it. At any rate it was the only source of mechanical power that Grannie availed herself of.

She worked from dawn to dark every day, usually outside the house except in the winter. She would build a fire in the back yard to heat the water for washing clothes, or to make soap—using wood ashes and waste lard—or to make apple butter or hominy. The hog butchering was also carried on in the back yard, with a stout pole put up between the clothesline posts for hanging the carcasses on. A couple of Grannie's sons would come and help her with the butchering, to be repaid with hog parts, like livers and hearts, that could not be cured.

By fall Grannie would have her kitchen rafters strung with drying red peppers and ears of corn, hams hung in the smokehouse, and jars of canned fruits and vegetables stacked row on row in the cellar. At our house most of these marks of industry and frugality were lacking. My father was making good wages as a carpenter in Neosho, and he brought most of our food home from there. It never seemed to me as tasty or interesting as Grannie's.

Speaking of my stepmother, Aunt Elda once said to Grannie in my presence, "Agnes doesn't seem to manage very well."

"Agnes couldn't manage a hog downhill," Grannie said, in one of the few remarks I ever remember her making.

She was usually taciturn to the point of near muteness, but then Ozarkers rarely talked to children, and that was one of the reasons my father and I were both considered a little odd. He had always responded to my natural volubility, though he began to try to dampen it a little when it became apparent that my stepmother resented our conversational rapport at meals. I soon learned to keep quiet at the table, and then I would go outside and talk to my father while he was doing chores or working with the bees. But my stepmother resented that, too, of course.

My father would sometimes say to her that he wished she could be kinder to me, and I was always sorry when he did. There was nothing she could do to me that I minded as much as I did his distress, or the tension his remarks about me created between the two of them, so I never did complain to him. But Agnes always imagined that that was what I was doing when I trailed my father around at his chores.

After I left home I used to visit my family on Sunday afternoons for the while they stayed near Joplin and more rarely after they moved back to Newton County. In spite of everything I remained homesick all the time I was in high school, and from the day I left home my stepmother and I became polite strangers, so that my visits were tolerable.

By the time I was in college, however, the other children and I had grown so far apart that I gave up the visits. Finally Agnes ran off to Colorado with another man, taking the children with her, and my father took his bees back to a little farm in Polk County, where I visited him regularly for the rest of his days.

I went back to my native Polk County neighborhood last fall and found that it hasn't at all changed in all these years. A six-lane highway to Kansas City now runs within a couple of miles of it, and it is only five miles from Bolivar, which has blossomed into a typical midwestern town, replete with filling stations, billboards, motels, and neon lights. But the road we traveled on when we moved when I was four is even hillier and more winding than I remembered it, though the distance between the two houses has been shortened to ten or fifteen minutes. Woodlawn School, which the older children in the family had attended before we moved and got too far away for them to walk to it, was still standing. Barren Creek Church (we had called it Barn Creek) which my father had been fatally remiss in not making his first set of stepchildren attend, had been rebuilt in stucco but on the same site and in the same dimensions—the old pews, built by my mother's first husband, are still in use and still fit in their places.

The sight of that road and those buildings last fall almost gave me a sensation of psychic claustrophobia. In my memory, that road, which led to every place in the whole big world, had been broad and romantic. The tiny school and church had been gracious, expansive buildings. To realize that the inner me—all of the inner me forever—had formed itself in those brief five years, when that road was my sole exit to the world and when Woodlawn School and Barn Creek Church were the grandest buildings I had ever seen, gave me an almost physical feeling of suffocation.

4

BISSLES AND BROCCOLI

The first house I was ever in that was equipped with store-bought rugs and bathrooms was one that I entered for the first time by the wrong door. It was a big, new, two-story red-brick house in the best residential section of Joplin, and I was there, the summer I was thirteen, to try out for a job as maid. Never having so much as even seen a servant before, I had no idea they were supposed to observe special rules of etiquette, so I was puzzled by the look of surprise my prospective employer gave me when she opened the door.

I said, "Mrs. Horton? Mrs. Ward said you told her I could come to work for you today."

Mrs. Horton was a vivacious-looking brunette with snapping brown eyes and gleaming teeth. She was probably in her early thirties but looked older because her figure was very unsuited to the styles of that day—in the late twenties. She had a very large bosom and slim hips and legs, and such figures, confined in the one-piece retaining garments of the day, descended in an unbroken line from the chest to the knee in about a forty-five-degree angle. This gave Mrs. Horton a premature grande-dame look that was more imposing than attractive.

She said, "Oh! You're Ethel. I was expecting you at the back door."

I was too innocent to regard the remark as a reprimand. I apologized and offered to go around and come in the right way. But Mrs. Horton said, "Never mind that now. Since you're here, you might as well come on in." Then she looked at me and noted that I was empty-handed. I hadn't yet acquired the habit of carrying a handbag—my streetcar fare was tied in the corner of a handkerchief in the pocket of my dress. "Didn't you bring anything to work in? You look so all-polished up it seems a shame to put you into a dirty kitchen," she said merrily.

I had on a stiffly starched blue cotton dress with a white collar, which I had carefully ironed myself, white stockings, and black patent-leather shoes. Mrs. Horton reminded me several times later of how I "positively glistened" that first day at her front door—"with those big china-blue eyes and that shiny blond hair. Even your face looked like you'd just given it a good rubbing with Bon Ami," she would say derisively. (Derision, I was to find, was the chief variation she made on her usual common-sense and businesslike manner toward me.)

Somehow it hadn't occurred to me to ask Mrs. Ward, a neighbor of ours who was Mrs. Horton's mother's cleaning woman, how things were done in houses like this. Mrs. Ward was the most high-toned, most fashionably dressed woman in our block in Chitwood, the slum of mine and smelter workers on the outskirts of Joplin where my family lived during the three years I was in the upper grades.

When we first moved there my father had a job on the

Frisco railroad, traveling in the division during the week as a carpenter on a maintenance crew. But the next year the unions went on strike and never went back to work, and when I was ready for high school my father was trying to support the seven children that were then his responsibility, and two recently orphaned neighbor children who had moved in with us, by doing carpentering odd jobs.

Mrs. Ward was the mother of Ronald Langdon, an ex-boyfriend of mine, whose father was one of the few men in our neighborhood who had a clean, safe job. Mr. Langdon was a member of the Joplin police force. Some time in the distant past Mrs. Ward had divorced him because, as she told me, he was "a loud-mouthed roughneck," resumed the name of her first husband and the father of her oldest son, took that son and her youngest Langdon son, and moved into a much nicer house a block away from the policeman's and become a career woman, cleaning rich people's houses. The policeman had married again, and Mrs. Ward still kept a maternal eye on Ronald, so he was in the interesting position of being under the daily supervision of two mothers.

But this was not the only reason I found him fascinating at first. He was lively and handsome and, as marks of his relatively bourgeois status, he wore knickers and shoes and stockings to school, and rode a bicycle. Most of the rest of us went barefooted to school except in the middle of winter, the other boys all wore denim overalls, and nobody else rode a bicycle. As the only boy I had seen up to then who resembled the boys in our primary readers, Ronald looked almost unbearably romantic to me, and I felt like the favorite of the gods when it became evident that he returned my regard. Ronald taught me

the city sidewalk and vacant-lot games: how to play jacks
and hopscotch, and how to roller-skate and ride a bicycle,
using his equipment.

The other children on our street played go-sheepie-go
and hide-and-go-seek on the nearby tailing piles—moun-
tainlike mounds of gravel from the lead and zinc mines
—and swam in the cave-ins. Fortunately, most of us had
learned to swim early at the safe end of the city park,
which was within walking distance, and there were few
drownings. Once in a game of tag on a tailing pile, I fell
and skidded on my knees down a sharp incline for about
twenty feet and landed in a sludge pond. But I swam
out with no ill effects but a badly skinned knee. That
took several months to heal because, or so the natives
said, the sludge had poisoned the wound, but it left me
with nothing worse than a lifelong scar.

A few of the old lead and zinc mines were still being
worked when we lived in Chitwood, and most of the fathers of those of my playmates who still had fathers
worked in them or in the nearby smelter. We played with
their discarded carbide lamps, and a play-medicine new
to me—croton oil—was added to our play-doctor kits. The
fathers were a fearsome and depressing lot, on the whole.
Most of them had a hacking cough, or a ghastly pallor, or
both, and they were listless and unfriendly around the
house, even when they were not sick in bed from lead
poisoning or from the effects of the croton oil they took
to cure the poisoning. My father would furiously lambaste
God and the capitalists every time one of the neighbor
men took sick or died, but children have no pity for un-
prepossessing adults. To me those doomed breadwinners
were just spectral presences who had perversely chosen
an unrewarding way of life.

My father would stubbornly hold out against working in the smelter himself, except when he had to use the job as a brief stopgap against a mounting grocery bill. My stepmother thought this was highhandedly self-regarding, and even I, precociously concerned about the family debts, sometimes had my doubts. But after a couple of weeks at the smelter, when my father began to take on the morose appearance and manner of the other men, I would become anxious for a carpentering job to open up so that he could get back to that more congenial trade.

Although Ronald's father had the advantage of looking cheerful and well fed, he was as inimical to children as the other fathers, so Ronald came to our house for me to help him with his themes and his long division, or to play.

Finally, when we were sitting in the swing on our front porch one day, Ronald asked me to be his girl. But, already a confirmed *bovaryste*, as the French call those of us who confuse literature and life, I regretfully declined in language straight out of the true-confession magazines which my stepmother had begun borrowing from the neighbors and which I, of course, had become absorbed in.

"No, Ronald," I said, with a sincerely felt bitterness, "I wish I could. But I am ten and a half and you are only ten, and it can never be."

He looked desolate, and I suddenly felt the barrier between us that the female creates when she has made the decision to reject a suitor. He felt it too, and got up to leave.

"You don't have to *go*," I said. "We can still be friends, but I don't think I should ride your bicycle any more."

We were in the fifth grade then, and at the end of the

next year, with the aid of the truant officer, I got a special promotion to the seventh grade and left Ronald behind for good.

All the other kids hated and feared the truant officer, but I regarded him as my secret ally. He was an old man with long white Santa Claus whiskers, and, although nearly everybody else in Chitwood drove cars of some kind, he still made his rounds in a one-horse buggy. In the country I had always stopped going to school when winter started and there were expensive shoes and outer clothing to buy, and even in the fall my stepmother had always made me stay home when there was extra work to do there. But now the truant officer was keeping me, and her two school-age children as well, in school most of the time.

I finally had an experience with the truant officer, though, that not only caused me to think of his Santa Claus appearance as arrantly fake but disillusioned me about expecting justice from representatives of the law. At that time I had injured a shinbone jumping off the fender of a moving car, and I was having periodic recurrences of pain and swelling.

People in Chitwood couldn't afford doctors for such minor disabilities, and mine was being treated by the application of poultices of egg white and alum. I wasn't so disabled that I couldn't iron, however, and one day I was alone in the house in the middle of a big ironing when I heard the truant officer's horse come clopping down the street.

He had bawled my stepmother out before for keeping me home to work while she "gadded about, gossiping with the neighbors," as he put it, so, forgetting my lame leg, I ran like a streak to the house next door, to warn her to hurry home. She wasn't there, though, so I ran back and got to our front door by the time the old man made it there.

"All right, Missy," he said. "Where is she?"

"I don't know," I told him.

"You're lying!" he shouted. "I seen you sneakin' out the back door to run over next door and tell her to hide when you seen me comin'."

I said, "No, I didn't. I thought she was there, and I was going to tell her to come home. But she had left."

"That's enough of your lies, now," he said. "I asked you a civil question and I expect a civil answer. Where's your mother? If she is your mother. She don't look like your mother to me, nor act it."

"She's my stepmother," I said, feeling defensive about her, as I often did. "And I answered you civilly. I said I don't know."

"A liar *and* a smart aleck!" he said. "I can see what you've been doing. Them clothes there didn't iron themselves. You tell that stepmother of yours, or whatever she is, that it's her place to do the ironin' and yours to be in school. And if you're not there tomorrow, she'll be in trouble. If you're able to iron, and to run back and forth to the neighbors', you're able to git to school."

Years later, doctors who X-rayed my leg for another reason discovered an extensive osteomyelitis scar on my shinbone and were amazed to learn that I hadn't known about it and that it had healed without treatment. It was horribly painful during the healing, though, but I limped to school the next day, feeling, that time, not gratitude but loathing for the truant officer.

The next year, I was put in the A-group of the eighth grade when school started and I got my diploma in Janu-

ary. From then until June I worked at home and vege-
tated, and then I knew I had to escape—to get back to
school.

I had first walked the three miles to a Joplin residential
district where the houses looked big enough to me that
I thought their owners could afford maids, but not so big
as to be overawing, and had started knocking on doors
at random. The only encouragement I had got was from
a friendly young housewife with a strange name, who
had told me she would talk to her husband about it. But
Mrs. Ward had discouraged me about that possibility.
She said, judging by the name, that the young woman
was Jewish and that Jews cooked with goose grease.

"You wouldn't even be able to eat things cooked with
that stuff," she told me, "much less cook them."

Then she told me she would help me find a place, and
a few days later, she reported hopeful results. She said
that the daughter of one of her ladies, a prominent society woman—"a richtocrat," Mrs. Ward explained—was
thinking of hiring a high-school girl. She wanted one,
however, that was old enough to take care of her five-
year-old son, and who could do the cooking and cleaning
for the family of three.

I was to be on trial, and was not very sanguine about
succeeding.

Washing dishes, however, was no novelty to me. I had
washed all the dishes at home since I was ten and the job
had fallen naturally to me when my last remaining older
half-sister, Blanche, had turned fifteen and got married.
But I had never seen anything like the dishes that confronted me now—stacks of them, all in perfect condition,
no chips or cracks, and all made of the most fragile materials imaginable. Mrs. Horton showed me where the

soap and the dishrag (which she called a dishcloth) were, and told me to wash the goblets and the tumblers first, "and be very careful of the stems."

I had never heard glasses called goblets and tumblers before, but I set to work, and Mrs. Horton told me she was going out and would be back for lunch, and that in the meanwhile I should finish the dishes, change the beds in the upstairs bedrooms, and, if there was any trash in the living-room floor, pick it up with the bissles. Her unnecessary cautionary remarks about the dishes almost proved to be my undoing. I washed and dried each goblet separately and set it carefully in its place on the shelf, and so on, through each delicate item. When Mrs. Horton returned, three hours later, I was just starting on the silverware.

"Good heavens!" she said. "Have you been in here all morning?"

I admitted that I had, offering no excuses.

"But I understood that you at *least* knew how to wash dishes. I'm just afraid this is not going to work out. You look like a big girl, but you *are* just a child, after all."

Mrs. Horton took over the dishwashing and I dried, with somewhat more dispatch than previously, and we worked in a heavy silence. Fortunately for me, the telephone soon rang, and it was a woman who had called while Mrs. Horton was out. The caller congratulated her on her intelligent, courteous, and efficient new maid and won me a second chance. I had made that impression by summoning up my hillbilly cordiality and politeness when the woman had asked for my employer. I had told her where she was and when she would be back, and asked if I could take a message, or if she wanted to leave her name or number. I probably hung on because I was grateful for hearing a human voice, after a couple of hours alone in that big house, but the caller turned out to be an important friend of Mrs. Horton's mother, and she was so sure that I was a paragon that I probably would have been able to get by for some time, doing nothing else but answering the telephone.

After lunch, Mrs. Horton went out again, and when she came home that evening she told me that everything was fine except that I hadn't swept up the trash in the living-room floor as she had told me to do. I had looked for the trash but I hadn't seen any—luckily, I thought, since I didn't know what bissles was—or were. I still couldn't see any trash till she pointed it out to me, and then I discovered that what she called trash was a couple snippets of thread and a few specks of lint, whereas I had been looking for something on the order of wads of old newspaper, bottle caps, and bread crusts. (The bissles turned out to be a carpet sweeper, trademarked Bissell's.)

The biggest change in my vocabulary was the addition of such housekeeping words, especially culinary ones. Within a couple of weeks I had learned the senses of: spatula, broccoli, Brussels sprouts, chives, soufflé, sauté, baste, tapioca, zwieback, aspic, croutons, blancmange, marinate, au gratin, casserole, coddle, and omelet. As I learned the words, I was learning to suit the actions to them, and, in spite of having no real interest in the art, I had become a very good cook by the time I was fourteen.

Mr. Horton, who was a gourmand, dampened my spirits one day when I was making a return trip from the kitchen with the biscuits, by remarking, "Ethel, if you ever make a writer, there's going to be a damn good cook

lost to the world." Mrs. Horton looked at him with an-
noyance. She disapproved of swear words.

It must have been my literary style of speech that misled Mrs. Horton as to my cultural tastes. Even after she
had met my father and stepmother in their natural setting, she held on to the illusion that I had sprung into the
world with a full-blown preference for the finer things
in life. She gave me their tickets to the Chicago Civic
Opera's performance of *Aida*—which is, I blush to admit,
the only opera I have ever attended—and to a road-com-
pany performance of *Hamlet,* with Robert Mantell and
Julia Marlowe in their farewell tour, for example. And
after every concert, or play, or art exhibit that she attended from a sense of duty, she would always say, "I
wish you had been there instead of me. You appreciate
things like that and I don't."

I made the second shift in dialect—from rural to urban
Ozarkese—without Mrs. Horton's noticing it. She always
considered me an egghead and a prig, which was all right
with me, because it caused her to keep her distance from
me, too. She told me once that she had never heard me
make a mistake in grammar, and that she knew I would
be a better influence on her small son (the only child
and my baby-sitting charge) than she was, because she
never could learn to parse sentences. I don't know why I
didn't confess to her that I was working hard to cure myself of talking "correct" grammar and to learn to talk as
she did. But I suppose I realized even then that explaining that would be awkward.

At first I supposed that there was one section of my
vocabulary that the Hortons were as ignorant of as I was
of theirs. Tom Howard, the five-year-old boy, had introduced me to a whole new set of euphemisms in that

area. He "went to the bathroom" to "grunt" or "wee-wee," or even, so delicate were his manners, to "go boom." But one day I was passing by the door of the living room, where he was playing with some other small boys, when he suddenly got up and said, "Excuse me, fellas. I've got to shit."

That opened up a whole new line of speculation for me as to what really went on beneath the immaculate Horton exterior. Still it didn't really prepare me for the worst. A year or so later, Tom Howard approached me one day and said he had something serious to discuss with me. "It's about Twyla," he said. Twyla was a high-school girl who lived with the Reinekes and whom I knew because Mr. Reineke was in business with Mr. Horton. The Reinekes' son was Tom Howard's age and they were playmates. The girl was of urban working-class origins and showed it—she dressed flashily, wore lipstick and high heels, and used low-class slang.

Tom Howard said, "Billy and I have decided Twyla is not a nice girl like you. We think she fucks with the boys."

I was so stunned that I was unable to do anything but chide my supposedly innocent little charge for using that word, though he must have thought I was remarkably temperate about it under the circumstances. Since I had heard it used among my age peers ever since I could remember, what struck me as really improper was that he would have spoken it in my presence, when my relationship to him was that of a surrogate parent.

All I said was, "You should never, never use that word when you're talking to someone older than you are, especially a girl."

He apologized and told me he had known he shouldn't say it, but that he and Billy had been anxious to get my opinion and he didn't know any other word to use. My opinion was that they were right, and I was as stunned by their perspicacity as anything else. But I considered it prudent to act as if I were too offended to say anything more.

There were several other girls, besides Twyla, who shared my maid-cum-student situation, but there was only one of them with whom I ever felt that I had anything else in common. That one was Lila Stone, who was beautiful and intelligent and who dressed in good taste, but who, at fourteen, was already soured on the world. She disdained to study and was impudent to her successive employers, and she refused to bring her lunch to school and eat it in the study hall at noon with the rest of us poor kids. However, when she lacked enough money to eat in the cafeteria, which was frequently, she was not above accepting half of my lunch, although Mrs. Horton always made sure that I didn't bring more than barely enough for myself.

Eventually I found out why Lila's various employers were willing to put up with her impudence and inefficiency. When Lila was born, Mrs. Horton told me, and for several years afterward, her parents had been on the fringes of the upper-upper Joplin social set and had mingled with the couples who were now taking on schoolgirl helpers. Then her father had failed in business and absconded, leaving Mrs. Stone with Lila and a still younger daughter.

At the time I knew Lila, she differed from us other student-maids in that her mother still lived in Joplin. Mrs. Stone was always moving from one small, tacky apartment to another, and I sometimes stopped with Lila to visit her as we were walking home from school.

Once as we approached a run-down old building that Lila's mother was then living in, we saw the town's only Rolls-Royce parked in front. Everybody knew that this conspicuous car belonged to Dan Page, the town's most flamboyant playboy. When Lila saw it, she said, "That son of a bitch. Come on. We're not going up." But just then Mr. Page came out of the building, patted Lila on the head and told her to be a good girl, and drove off.

Mrs. Stone, who was usually overjoyed to see us, was in tears when she answered Lila's knock at the door that day, and she told us to go away.

After that Lila took me with her a couple of times to Mr. Page's office to ask him for money to buy something she needed, such as shoes or a coat. After we left, she would cuss the man out for being a chinchy tightwad and excoriate her mother for being too easy on him.

I had always been depressed by the visits to Mrs. Stone, a harried-looking, faded, but still attractive redhead. She constantly embarrassed me by holding me up as a model of conduct to Lila, and by expressing her profuse gratitude to me for being so kind to her unworthy child. My natural affinity for outcasts had gotten me into the same sort of uncomfortable relationships several times before, and I began to think that the greatest danger in befriending the underdog lay in incurring the gratitude of the underdog mothers.

When I was in the second grade, the year we lived in the Red House, I had let an unattractive little girl named Lydia Landsaw use my drinking cup at every recess. The cup was a silver-plated, collapsible affair that had been in the family for several years, and I was allowed to take it to school when the teacher, who was considered a health nut, decided to make the unprecedented ruling that we pupils could no longer share the dipper in the water bucket but had to bring our own cups. Besides being the poorest child in the school, Lydia was the one with least charm, and I was the only one who would play with her during recess. After watching her pass up her turn at the water bucket a couple of times, I had started slipping my folding cup to her, either before or after I had used it, according to which one of us was first in line. Lydia was such a woebegone mess that I felt that letting her use my cup was a true sacrifice, especially after Miss Schaffer's lurid accounts of the multiplicity of oral bacteria. But I would no doubt have forgotten Lydia by now except for a harrowing scene her mother put me through later. At Christmastime, after I had already stopped going to school for that year, a wagon, driven by a strange woman, with two or three strange children in the back, pulled up in front of our house. Women drivers of any kind were anomalies in those days, and this one, oddly dressed and driving an old farm wagon, made an especially queer sight. My stepmother started down the path to see why the woman had stopped, but the stranger said she wanted to talk to me.

I went reluctantly out to the wagon, and the woman lifted me up onto the seat beside her. Then she told me that I had been so kind to her poor, stupid, fatherless little girl that neither of them would ever forget me. She said that she had wanted to do something to repay me but that she hadn't been able to afford it.

"I've brought you a little present," she said. "It ain't much but it took ever cent I could spend for Christmas." I opened it. It was a five-cent pencil and a ten-cent tablet. I was silent, my impulse being to return the gifts.

But my stepmother, who was standing by, said, "Ethel, where's your manners?"

So I thanked the woman briefly, scrambled down, and ran into the house. I was given to writing letters then to be enclosed with the letters that anybody else wrote to our Polk County and California relatives, but I didn't have the heart to use Mrs. Landsaw's gifts until a long time later, when the memory of the embarrassing scene had faded.

I recall one unpleasant episode with Lila Stone that did not involve her mother. The memory of this one has often recurred to me because it was the first of several experiences I have had that indicate that I have a tendency toward selective amnesia. It occurred one day when Lila was sharing my lunch in the study hall and asked to borrow my pen to finish a theme for English class. I had left my pen in my purse, which was in my locker, so I gave her the key and told her to go get it. Pretty soon she returned with the purse and said she had preferred not to open it. This delicacy seemed a little odd in Lila at the time, but it didn't impress me especially until the next day when I looked in the purse to get the four dollars and fifty cents I had been saving up all year to pay for a copy of the school annual, and found the money compartment empty.

That evening I recounted this sequence of events to Mrs. Horton and she agreed that I had cause to be suspicious. For a few days after that I was cool to Lila, but by another month or so, we had resumed our old palship. Then a new employer of Lila's who was visiting Mrs. Horton remarked that she suspected that someone was making unauthorized purchases on her charge accounts, and Mrs. Horton called me in to repeat the story of what had happened to my money. I honestly didn't know what she was talking about.

She prodded my memory, step by step, and as she did I remembered it all, but I don't think either of the women believed me by that time.

Lila didn't return to high school the next year. She got a job as ticket seller at the Orpheum, and started wearing makeup and high heels. She looked very glamorous and self-satisfied in her little cage, and when I had scraped together thirty-five cents and would count it out for her in exchange for a ticket, she would slide one through to me with a remote and disdainful smile. But I was just as sure that she was the one who was throwing her life away.

My reputation as a paragon among the small, marked group of student-girl workers was something I much preferred not to be reminded of. In the role of an industrious, conscientious maid and a dedicated student, I regarded myself as a fraud. It couldn't be denied that I was doing all the cooking, dishwashing, and ironing for the Hortons, and cleaning their eight-room house by myself on Saturdays. Nor that at school I was keeping on the honor roll in spite of taking five solids so that I could finish early, while also working on the staff of the paper and debating.

But my guilty secret was that I was spending at least half of my time when I wasn't in school in extracurricular reading. That compulsion had not abated. In that pursuit, my reputation as a slow worker, which my father, with characteristic candor and honesty, had passed on to my employer, and which my first week as a maid had confirmed, stood me in good stead. During my first year at the Hortons' I had read the Bible from cover to cover, all of Shakespeare's plays, and about half of the complete

set of the Book of Knowledge, including the phonetic
lessons in French, besides keeping up with the magazines
at hand—*Collier's, Redbook, Good Housekeeping, Cosmo-
politan,* and the *National Geographic.* I kept ahead of the
necessary reading for school by going rapidly through all
the textbooks that were at all readable when I first got
them and then getting by on what I remembered. I got
my Latin or French by dashing to class and running
through the vocabulary and inflections while the rest of
the students were straggling in; I worked my algebra or
geometry problems on the streetcar, on the way to school.

I bought secondhand textbooks, trading them in at the
end of each term, never regarding the books themselves
as valuable possessions. In fact I never did acquire the
urge to own books that seems to be natural to my fellow
booklovers, and I suspect this void in my bundle of ac-
quisitive instincts is traceable to unpleasant memories
connected with the ownership of the first two books I
ever considered mine. The first one was a small beautiful
book containing the lyrics of an old song, "Bingen on the
Rhine," with illustrations. The song was one of those my
father sang to us children at bedtime as we gathered
around and listened while he rocked the youngest one
to sleep. He had seen the festively bound booklet in the
dime store in Neosho during the Christmas season and
he brought it to me on my seventh birthday. It was a sad
song about a dying soldier, and my father had taken advantage of my questions about it to try to enlighten us
about wartime enemies. I found that my heart still melted
with pity for the mortally wounded young man, even
after I had learned the disconcerting fact that he was a
countryman of Old Kaiser Bill, who figured in a merrily
murderous ditty I had learned from my schoolmates.

I treasured my book for about half an hour, the time it took my stepmother to get supper on the table. Then she refused to sit down and eat, and my father saw his error. He explained that the book was really for everybody, but that he had given me custody of it because I could read it, and because it was my birthday. I didn't understand that kind of ownership, but I knew I should help my father rectify his mistake. After supper, I put the book among the family-owned hymn books in the organ box, and I never looked at it again except secretly. Several months later I took it out one day and saw that there was a yellow stain, like a rain streak, across its pure-white moiré cover. After that I mentally disowned it. The little kids marked on it and tore out its pages, and I didn't care. I had all the words and the pictures stored in my brain, where nobody could get at them.

The second book I briefly owned was a Latin textbook, when I was twelve. The city schools furnished textbooks through the eighth grade, the grade I was in then, but I was in the junior high school that year and got special permission to take Latin, a ninth-grade subject. I felt I had no right to ask my parents to indulge me in this luxury, even if they could have afforded the price of the book, so I got by for the first month by hastily going over the lesson in another student's book while the class was convening. I made a hundred on the first test, but the next day the teacher presented me with a brand-new textbook which she said had been bought for me by Miss Viola Smoot, one of her fellow teachers whom I knew only by sight. I felt betrayed again—it flashed through my mind that the teachers must have been discussing me in a meeting—and I declined the gift. But the Latin teacher told me I would have to have a book or drop the course, so I accepted it as the lesser of two evils. I left the book with the Latin teacher at the end of the term, but that did not, of course, restore the balance between me and the Lady Bountiful who had bought it for me. For her two dollars and a half, she had bought the right to patronize me all through high school, as well as when I returned to teach in the same system with her seven years after having accepted her charity. Or so I always felt.

I managed to do all that reading *and* the housework at home by becoming a secret speed demon at the housework. My employer, a dedicated clubwoman and bridge and golf player, was never at home during the daytime, so I would read first and work later. I discovered that I could iron a boy's shirt in five minutes and a man's shirt in ten, so I allowed myself exactly an hour and a half for the twelve shirts I had to iron on Wednesdays. I could clean the eight-room house in half the time Mrs. Horton thought it was taking me, so I would spend a hectic three or four hours on Saturday afternoons at the job after reading all Saturday morning. My conscience would sometimes bother me when my employer would come home in the evenings and commiserate with me for having had to drudge all day because I was so slow, but I still craftily concealed my change of habits from her. She paid me two dollars a week besides my board and room, and she expected me to earn it by putting all of my out-of-school time at her disposal. She always found floors to polish or windows to wash if I got through with my regular chores while she was at home. I once absent-mindedly gave away one of my typical short cuts when she was talking to me while I was ironing. I was shortening shirt-ironing time by about a minute per shirt by running the iron over the damp, starched collars and cuffs, and then pressing them with my hand against an enameled tabletop right behind the ironing board so that the steam condensed and dried them out. Mrs. Horton was duly impressed with my inventiveness, but wondered why I wasn't applying it to the other areas of housekeeping. If she had only known. I developed enough tricks during my stint as a maid to keep Heloise Cruse busy for a week, and I've often been tempted to do so.

I gratefully abandoned housekeeping forever, though, after two more years of part-time maid work at college, so it was the other things I picked up in that house— chiefly a thorough indoctrination in middle-class manners and attitudes—that had the lasting effect on me.

Still, my brief renown as an expert cook rises to haunt me occasionally even now. I have run for office, led civic drives, served on boards, and been listed in black and white in the local newspaper among "leading citizens." But there is one rich old bore in our town whom I occasionally run into, at the sort of huge affairs that people like him and me are both invited to, who knows nothing about me except that I am a whiz at barbecuing something or other—hamburgers, I think. I always manage to find somebody else to talk to just before he gets to the meat of his subject. Every time he sees me, his eyes light up. "Ah, you're the little girl that used to live with Diana when you were going out here to the teachers' college. You remember the night you fixed those barbecued—" I don't even remember how to barbecue, let alone that party, and I suppose it's the old selective amnesia again.

But my working knowledge of middle-class domestic

manners and habits has stayed with me. In the maid's uniform I wore at my employers' parties—black dress, white apron, with a white lace doily tied atop my head— I was invisible to most of the guests. (The barbecue fiend was an exception.) But, in my capacity as a writer, I was studying them carefully. And, much as I detested the work involved, I understood how useful the opportunity to observe those types at firsthand would be to me. I never really felt more involved in my role than if I had chosen instead to masquerade as a criminal to study life in a prison. And I had no more desire to trade places with the objects of my scrutiny than if that had been the case.

I had no doubts that the feeling was mutual, of course. Years later, one of the men who was sometimes among the Hortons' guests said to me, "Mildred and Jim Horton must have been terribly embarrassed to have someone so superior to them acting as a servant in their house."

But of course they never were. Nobody—at least nobody in the Middlewest—ever feels snobbish about anything but inherited wealth, and nobody ever feels inferior to anybody else except to those who have more of it.

5

THE TOT AS BRAINWASHER

After six years of being on my own and ostensibly a free agent, I found myself at nineteen transformed into an elementary school teacher, a role that had lost all its appeal for me by the time I was in the fifth grade. (The "life certificate" I had just been issued by a teachers' college for having completed the equivalent of three years of higher education had an ominous sound for me.)

The series of events that had boxed me into that cul-de-sac began when the Joplin high school principal had thrust an unsolicited scholarship to the teachers' college upon me at the end of my first semester at the Bolivar Baptist junior college. Although I had finished the required number of high school courses in the winter, I had had to go back to Joplin in the spring to get my diploma with my class, and Mrs. Horton told me that she had accepted in my name one of the small scholarships I had been offered as the graduate with the fifth highest grades. In Bolivar I had acquired the social status of my mother's family, who were in good standing in top Republican and Baptist circles, and I had been appointed editor of the college annual for the next year and had been elected president of the best literary-social club. I didn't want to go back to living in a maid's room; I didn't want to change colleges; and I didn't want to be a teacher, but the scholarship was the only sure way I saw of getting the money to pay my fees at any college.

So I reluctantly found a mother's-helper job in Springfield and enrolled at the teachers' college. On my first college job, I not only did all the chores I was doing at the Hortons', including baby-sitting with a little girl, but was also given the job of doing the family laundry—on an old-fashioned washboard in old-fashioned tubs. But after a month or so I became friendly with a middle-aged childless couple next door who were building a big new house in the swankest part of town. I gladly accepted their invitation to move with them. The Houks had a part-time maid who did all the cleaning, including my room, and all the laundry, including mine. They treated me as a member of the family, and talked about adoption, but Mrs. Houk was a very possessive, domineering woman, and could have offered me nothing at that time that would have induced me to surrender my independence. I said I would continue to live in their house only if it was on a quid-pro-quo basis, so they let me get breakfast in the mornings and help at their frequent parties. (It was one of their guests whom I impressed with my barbecuing skill.) I lived with the Houks, reading better books and magazines and hearing better talk than I had theretofore been used to, for the two years it took me to get my teaching certificate and a job.

When I entered the teachers' college, my plans had been to have as little as I could to do with the education courses and to take all the courses I could get in literature and languages, perhaps preparing to teach high school

English, if I had to, as a side line to my writing career. During my sophomore year, however, when I had to get my major approved by Dr. Virginia Craig, the head of the English department, that brilliant and perceptive woman turned me down.

"To be a good teacher of English," she said, "you have to be capable of a vast amount of very hard work. And *you* are not. Everything has been too easy for you."

I was astounded. Not that I didn't think she was right. What amazed me was that she knew. I was then taking my third English course under her, and I had been getting the highest grades in her class. I could only guess that she had divined my cynical and frivolous attitude toward classwork and textbooks from the weekly column I was writing in the student newspaper. Nevertheless I was desolate at having my plans wrecked, and I mentally blamed all those gullible teachers before this nemesis who had fostered my habit of sliding by without studying by giving me top grades for such little effort. I thought I might salvage something from the wreck by suggesting that I go on studying English, regardless of what sucker I might subsequently induce to approve me for a major in his department. But Dr. Craig rejected that suggestion, too.

"We're taking up grammar next," she said, "and you don't need it. You probably already know more about grammar than the author of the textbook. It would offer no challenge to you."

I was overwhelmed with self-pity at the thought that the sins of my early childhood and the imperceptiveness of my former teachers were catching up with me at this crucial point in my life.

I tried to keep my composure, and I did manage to blink back the tears, but this caused my nose to start running, and I hadn't brought a handkerchief. In that emergency, I backed hurriedly out of Dr. Craig's office, sniffling and speechless, realizing that I had been at last exposed for the fraud I was, and feeling that my life was ruined.

I stopped in a rest room around the corner, blew my nose on some toilet paper, composed myself, and rushed to the office of the head of the history department, hoping to get him committed before the word got around. That unsuspecting soul said he would be delighted to have such a brilliant student as I majoring in his subject and signed my card. But, after thinking it all over, I decided that the only honest thing for me to do was to switch to elementary school teaching, which, or so I judged from the elementary school teachers I had observed, any slob could do. And, after all, there was a depression on. I had to do *something*.

By the next summer I had earned my life certificate and signed up with a teachers' employment agency. The jobs out West and those in such outposts as Hawaii and Alaska appealed to me most, but they all stipulated that applicants must be at least twenty-five years old or married. Finally I was reduced to applying at Joplin, and the superintendent hired me on the spot. However, he spoiled any sense of triumph I might have felt by congratulating himself on his charity.

He was a smug-looking man at best, and so fat that his jowls always quivered impressively after he had made an emphatic point during a speech before the student body. In fact some of us students had made a game of guessing when he was making a point that was going to be weighty enough, in his own opinion, to warrant a good waddling of his jowls at us to punctuate it.

He must have been flattered with the rapt attention I was giving his every word during the job interview. But in spite of myself, and with growing horror at how I might react when it happened, I was absorbed in awaiting the opportunity to study the jowl-waddling phenomenon up close.

He concluded the interview by saying in his most pompous manner, "The greatest pleasure I get out of this job is in being able to help deserving, hard-working girls by starting them out on their careers as teachers—the greatest, most noble calling on this earth!" Then it came, as I had expected. But his words were so dispiriting and so guilt-provoking that I looked away, and of course lost any inclination I might have had to giggle.

I devoted my full energies to the teaching job. Grannie Ware once told me, when I was giving her some unsolicited aid in some chore, that I always went at everything like I was killin' snakes, and that's how I went at teaching. I was at the school by eight every morning and worked till dusk, and I felt rewarded by the results. Within a few months, my pupils were not only getting top scores in system-wide achievement tests, but were collecting the most tinfoil for the Red Cross and selling the most PTA memberships.

By the end of my first year at teaching, however, I was beginning to see that personal satisfaction was about all I was going to get out of the job. The other teachers resented me as an eager beaver, and the supervisors showed more displeasure at my—to them—unorthodox teaching methods than pleasure at the results.

At teachers' college, I had been taught progressive

methods and I believed (and still believe) that they were best. What I had come away with that I could use were a few broad principles—that a child learns by doing, and in response to felt needs; that you educate the whole child; that individual differences must be taken into account; that children are not robots and will learn better and behave better if they are not treated as such.

The principal at my first school was a short, fat, peppery Irishwoman who conducted her own classes as a strict disciplinarian but was not much concerned about how her staff conducted their classes, so long as they kept reasonable order, and so long as their pupils showed reasonable progress on the achievement tests that were given periodically by the system supervisors.

At first she would look a little dubious when she came in to my room, say during art class, to find half the pupils out of their seats—some gathered around a table in the front of the room, working on a group mural, others on their way to or from my desk where materials were spread out so they could choose their own. The usual thing in art classes those days was for pupils to sit at their desks and all work on the same thing at the same time, as teacher demonstrated. Still, Miss Carney was delighted with what my pupils came up with in art and composition, and there was no arguing with their achievement records in the tests on skills. So she let me go my own way.

That first year of teaching I was at a school in one of the poorer parts of town, only a cut above Chitwood. I was assigned to the fifth grade and, because some of the boys were rather large and rough-looking and I was only nineteen, I was afraid I would have disciplinary problems. I had none at all the first semester, but the second semester I had one wished on me.

Miss Northcutt, who taught the fourth grade and was also a beginner, was having all sorts of problems with discipline, the worst of them with Albert Boyer, who was twelve years old and hated school. Miss Northcutt paddled him regularly—at least once a day. At the beginning of the second semester the principal decided that it would be best for all concerned if she put Albert in my room, where the children were a year nearer his age.

Miss Northcutt was a graduate of a liberal arts college and was mainly trying to get by on her memory of educational methods. I was having to do a great deal of adaptation to fit the progressive tenets I had learned in with the demands of the supervisors and the principal, and in order to use the textbooks I was furnished. But one thing that certainly had no place in my educational philosophy was corporal punishment.

I concluded that Albert Boyer was misbehaving to get attention. His parents were elderly and old-fashioned and dressed him in tight knee breeches (obviously cut down from something else) and long stockings, while the other boys wore overalls and socks. Albert's hair always needed cutting, and he was pale and underweight. He had two older brothers, both in the penitentiary. But Albert, I knew, had an above-normal IQ and I decided to act on the premise that he could be reached by the exercise of reason.

My first project, therefore, was to remove the attraction of his misbehavior for him by absolutely ignoring it. When he drew a caricature of me at the blackboard where he was supposed to be working an arithmetic problem, I looked at it with interest, showed him where his proportions were wrong, and told him to go over to a side board, where he wouldn't disturb the other children, and try to improve it. He did, and turned out some fair work, then soon lost interest.

After a few days of this sort of byplay, Albert discovered how he could force me to abandon my attitude of indifference. He started attacking the other children physically. One day as the class was filing out for recess, he grabbed the hair of a little girl in front of him and gave it a vicious yank. I said nothing then, but I simmered all during recess, at the same time trying to plan a nice reasonable speech to make to Albert later. When the children were all seated again, I got a grip on myself and said, before all the class: "Albert, what would you do if you were a teacher and had a boy in your class who was so determined to be the meanest boy in school that he tortured other little children, just to get attention? Suppose you were the teacher, and had to protect the children from a boy like that, and you saw him hurt another child just to force you to do something, what would you do?"

Albert slowly rose, as if to recite, looked at me sardonically for a moment, then drawled, "Git red in the face, like you're a-doin', I reckon." The other children all roared with laughter, partly from shock, and I realized my mistake. I shouldn't have provided Albert with an audience. However, I managed a small rueful smile myself and dropped the problem for the moment.

Albert never repeated the torture gambit, however, and I began to outmaneuver him by forcing him into the role of the good boy. I sent him on errands, ordered him to help the slower students, asked him to sit at my desk and keep order when I had to leave the room, etc. Finally I told him if he worked ahead in the textbooks I would put him into the sixth grade with the other children of his age where he should have been, and he began to do so.

The principal taught the sixth grade, and she was a good teacher and disciplinarian with a great deal of experience. In her room Albert continued to be a model student, and he went on to junior high the next year with the rest of his age group and through high school with no further difficulty. He had been domesticated.

Albert was a good thing to have had happen to me in my first year. The next year I was transferred to the school in Joplin's wealthiest section—the Hortons' old neighborhood—and I came with reinforced faith in rational and humane teaching methods. Scattered among those children of privilege were others whose parents were squatters on abandoned mining land beyond the developed residential area, and they included some problem children that made Albert look tame by comparison.

During my first semester at the new school I functioned below par because of a personality problem of my own. At that school I was teaching English and physical education to all three upper grades and I had to deal with every little snob in the school. But I eventually decided I was wrong in thinking the little snobs had any inclination to snub me.

Jane Lanphier, the haughtiest little girl in the school, accidentally set me straight on that. Jane took ballet lessons from Miss Kirtley, as had all the little girls in her social group for generations, and her mother volunteered Jane's services for the first PTA program I had to present.

Jane was short and plump and didn't dance very well, but she tried hard, and after the program, when I was helping her off with her tutu, I impulsively forgot my hostility, gave her a little hug, and thanked her.

A few days later, Mrs. Lanphier, a snob of the highest

order, came to see me. She said that Jane had come home that night deliriously happy and finally told her why. "You won't believe it, Mother," Jane had said, "but guess what! Miss Reed kissed me!"

My problems after that were not with the children but with the principal and the other teachers, who continued to be on the lookout for slights from the parents or the students, and who imagined that my developing rapport with them was due to my having learned a special technique of catering to them. But it was really just that as soon as I found out that the pupils were not blocked, receptively, by feelings of superiority to me, their actual social superiority ceased to concern me.

At this school, the principal was truly scandalized by my classroom methods. The appearance of absolute order was all that she was after, and she was sure that no good would come of my permissive attitude. In her school, the plateau system was in effect—the pupils went from one room to another for various subjects—and when the bell rang, on the hour, I was accustomed just to let them go. The principal soon set me straight on that. She instructed me that when the bell rang I was to say, "Turn" (pause). "Rise" (pause). "Pass." On the first command, the pupils were to swivel to their left in their seats, wait for the second command, then stand, then wait for the third command, then file to the back of the room and fall in line.

That principal's ideas of how to teach subject-matter similarly emphasized order and routine, and she started visiting my room frequently to get me in line. Unfortunately, my pupils, especially the A, or high-IQ fourth-grade group in my home room, seemed bent on confirming her worst suspicions about where my permissiveness was bound to lead.

One day she was there during good-conduct class—she believed that even good conduct could be taught best by reading and writing about it, and we had workbooks on the subject—when it came the turn of Elinor Flick to recite. Elinor, a blond child with an angelic look and a genius IQ, was to read her written answer to the question, "Have you ever been rude? State the occasion. Why do you now think that what you did was rude?"

Elinor read, "Last week Miss Reed took our class on a field trip to see the waterworks. As we were walking by a house, I looked up and saw a pregnant woman on her porch watching us. I said to the girl who was walking with me, 'Oh, look, Joan! There's a lady who's going to have a baby.' As soon as we were past the house, Miss Reed said, 'Elinor, you shouldn't make remarks about anyone's appearance. It's rude.' If the woman had already had her baby and I had said, 'Look, Joan, there's a tiny baby!' I don't believe it would have been rude. I think now there must be something funny about getting pregnant that I don't understand, but that I hope to find out about, and that this makes it seem rude to comment on pregnancy.

"The reason I think that I was rude then is that Miss Reed told me I was."

Miss Macdonald was, of course, horrified. She set up appointments with first Elinor and then me after school. I saw Elinor, the self-confident—Elinor, the imperturbable—Elinor, the golden child—whose serenity I had feared to disturb—come out of Miss Macdonald's office in tears, ignoring my presence, as I waited to go in.

Miss Macdonald told me that if I had instilled the proper respect in my students I would have avoided such impertinences as Elinor's, who obviously knew that her remarks had been lewd and indecent and had been testing me out to see how far she could go. I insisted that Elinor's parents, who were college graduates and notorious avant-gardists, had probably wanted to protect Elinor from any idea that pregnancy was obscene, and that I would have been exceeding my authority to disregard their wishes. My conference ended with the principal's instructions to me that I must start being firmer in my discipline and that, besides, I should start doing my hair up.

I did put my Garbo bob up in a bun the next day, but I was determined not to change my teaching methods.

Another time, shortly after that, one of my physical-education classes was filing from my room to the next one when I noticed some tittering at the back of the row.

"What's going on there?" I asked one of the boys.

"Old Jack'll show you," the boy said.

"All right, Jack," I said. "What's so funny?"

Jack lowered his books, which he had been carrying clutched to his chest, and said, "Look. Miss Matthews."

Miss Matthews, who was the arithmetic teacher, was a tall, slender young woman with a remarkable bosom. Jack had created the diversion by stuffing two large wads of wastepaper into his sweater.

I regarded the prank as of no more significance than if he had pretended to be walking on high heels or wearing a funny hat, and I just ordered him to put his stuffing in the wastebasket, where it belonged, and to stop the horseplay.

About ten minutes later I was summoned to the principal's office again. Miss Macdonald was sitting at her desk in a state of white-lipped shock and anger, across from her Miss Matthews was sobbing hysterically and

Jack was cowering guiltily in his chair. Miss Macdonald ordered me to explain what had taken place. It seemed that the stir of amusement had persisted until the class reached Miss Matthews' room down the hall and that she had also investigated its source.

Both Miss Matthews and Miss Macdonald regarded Jack and me as equally culpable, my casual attitude about the crime being at least as reprehensible as Jack's dirty mind. Miss Macdonald told me that I should have punished the boy, and that, since I hadn't done so, she would have to. It was in the depth of the depression and I should have considered survival first, but I was foolhardy enough to tell the principal that if she whipped Jack for what he had done, I would resign that moment. I walked out after that daredevilish announcement and Miss Macdonald didn't whip the boy, but she lectured him for an hour—on what I can't imagine even now—and shortly after the episode I was asked to report to the superintendent's office.

The superintendent told me that I had been reported for "insubordination" and asked me to give my version of the incident that had brought the report about.

I refused. I told him that a conflict of personalities and attitudes was involved and that I couldn't say anything that would justify my point of view in the eyes of the principal, and that what I could say now would only sound like further insubordination. Then I stood up to go. I thought that if he couldn't see that Miss Macdonald was a neurotic old maid, it would do no good to tell him.

The superintendent said, "Well, Miss Reed, I called you in here to give you an opportunity to explain, and if you refuse to do so, I'm afraid there's nothing I can do for you."

I said, "I understand that," and left.

I couldn't have done anything else if I had been sure I would starve as a result, and I rather thought I might. I didn't know then and I can't be sure now, in contemplating that act of defiance or several others that followed, whether my conduct was due to a compulsion to put principle above survival or to a deeper impulse toward self-destruction, but, in any case, I had no regrets. On the contrary, I rather enjoyed the suspense.

When contract-signing time came around that spring, I wasn't given one. I was notified instead that I was on probation. After that Miss Macdonald put up with me for two more years, and then I was notified that I was being transferred back to my first school. I was glad about that, but one more year there, with all the freedom to conduct my classes in my own way, only convinced me finally that schoolteaching, with or without restrictions, was not my métier. I enjoyed the actual teaching but detested my social role and I was discouraged by the lack of financial rewards, or even of recognition, for special effort and achievement, and, when school was out that year, I quit.

I still don't know what can be done about rewarding superior teachers. I worked until dark every day—tutoring children with speech defects, or nonreaders, or those with other problems, planning projects, etc. I suppose I owed my job, at a time when jobs were so scarce and I was so young, to the scores my pupils made on achievement tests and to my popularity with the parents. But if it had been up to my immediate superiors and my colleagues to rate me, salary-wise, I don't think I would ever have been promoted. In fact, they continued to find my eager-beaverness annoying and, since they judged any teacher's proficiency mainly by how subdued she kept her pupils, they were highly dubious about my skill at that.

I wouldn't trust the kind of people who usually get into school administration to judge the actual merit of teachers. Too many of them are impressed by the wrong things. Besides, even achievement tests of the pupils will not tell the whole story on their progress. Teachers do educate the whole child, and the Albert Boyers they can rescue—or prevent from developing—should be chalked up to their credit. And who can pinpoint such cases?

In short, I don't believe there is any equitable way to institute merit pay for teachers in a socialized school system. Nor do I have much hope that anything else can be done that will assure attracting better people to the field. By "better" is usually meant more intelligent, more ambitious, more adaptable. But intelligent, ambitious, and adaptable people can succeed at less restricting vocations—and their intelligence assures that they will have observed the limitations of the teaching profession from at least the third grade on.

There are other "good" qualities, anyway, that even adequate teachers excel in. Above all, they need patience, kind hearts, and a capacity for deluding themselves as to the importance of trivia. Intelligence may not be incompatible with the first two of these, but it probably is with the third. It may not be true that slow learners make the best teachers but they are certainly capable of greater empathy with those under their tutelage who need empathy most.

H. L. Mencken proposed that teaching should be left to the dedicated asses—that people equipped to succeed at something else should leave them an open field. Without any premeditation, this is more or less what actually happens, and it is probably a good thing.

Oddly enough, it is probably those of us not called to the vocation, who got into it by force of circumstances during the Depression who are responsible for the twenty-year fling of Dewey progressivism—which the intellectuals are now seeing as anti-intellectual—in the public schools. Intellectuals in the thirties took teaching jobs because they had college degrees and then they went on to professorships in schools of education and administrative jobs in public school systems through natural momentum, and, in the opinion of some, wrought havoc.

It was they—the intellectual males in positions of power and (especially) the intellectual females in the lower echelons—who were most ready to discount the social and economic value of intellectuality. They had good reason, having had some experience with it. If they put exceptionally high intelligence among the physical and emotional handicaps, it was from bitter knowledge.

Thus arose the paradox that has ever since puzzled the intelligent outsider who examines the philosophy of American educators: the apparent anti-intellectualism of the intellectuals. The true scholar/intellectual has been the advocate of courses in hairdressing and auto mechanics (instead of Latin and algebra) because he knows the former would be more useful. From bitter experience, he has learned that the chief value of Latin and algebra is the pleasure they give as ends in themselves to people who enjoy things like Latin and algebra.

The chief advocates of "mental disciplines" for everyone, on the other hand, are those who did not enjoy Latin and algebra and who, consequently, probably know very little about either. Among them are most school superintendents and most school-board members—practical, non-intellectual men—who believe that the unpleasantness they endured while being subjected to the "mental disciplines" helped to build their sturdy characters.

The intellectuals who got into the school systems, for want of something better during the Depression, were attracted by the Dewey "life adjustment" theories out of humaneness. As sincere altruists they could not honestly act, in their role as educators, as if intellectuality would be a desirable attainment in our society. Possessing it, they had learned to prize it less than those who don't even recognize it when they see it.

Before the end of my first year at teaching, I was aware that the role was doing something to me that I didn't like, and I had no hopes that time would improve things. As a book reader, I suspected that there was good reason for the stereotype of the schoolmaster—altered only in irrelevant details for the schoolmarm—that has persisted since the first one stepped before the first group of *discipuli* and assumed his role (or rather, had his role thrust upon him). What happens to a person who unwarily puts himself in that position could, I think, best be explained by the Jungian psychologists, since it seems to set off a chain of atavistic human reactions that reinforce each other. At any rate, I believe the effects are irreversible.

How long the process takes hasn't been determined, but I can attest from personal experience that five years is more than adequate, at least when that exposure is added to the preconditioning of teacher training. A good many years after I had ended my five-year stint in a classroom in the teacher role, a pre-schooler whom I, in the role of friendly neighbor, was teaching to tie his shoes, unmasked me in less than three minutes. He submitted to my ministrations, executed his first bowknot, then established that peculiar gulf between us by labeling me instead of thanking me: "You're a schoolteacher, aren't you?"

Teachers themselves eventually become aware that some irresistible force is pushing them into a mold, but they rarely recognize that force for what it is. A fourth of a group of Missouri teachers who were polled on job attitudes a few years ago indicated that they felt their personal and social lives were being "inhibited," but the best they could do toward identifying what was working on them was to refer to it as "indirect pressures."

Fortunately for the survival of the institution of public education, teachers who chafe at such restraints are likely to go through life under the delusion that the "pressures" spring from the transient whims of the local PTA or school board and may disappear with time or a change of milieu.

They ignore such portents of the timelessness of their role as the nature of the schoolmasters in classical literature, and the fact that the word "pedant" already had its derogatory connotations when Samuel Butler used it. They do not ask how it happens that "schoolmasterly" (i.e., its Gallic equivalent) meant the same thing to Montaigne four hundred years ago as it means to us today. But what the durability of the stereotype suggests to those less inclined to shut their eyes to the implications is that there is something inherent in the calling—something that antedated PTAs and school boards by a few millennia —that ineluctably transforms normal people who are exposed to it into schoolmasterly types.

Tracing the thing back to its elemental origins is a job for the Jungians, but there is clearly a latent emotional pattern in the mass human mind that is triggered into activity by confrontation with an adult in a certain type of quasi-ceremonial *ambiance*. The subject needs only to be facing the group across a small barrier (table, desk, pulpit, podium) on which he may rest the vessels (books, chalice, bottles, silk hat) and wands (pointers, batons, yardsticks) he uses in his incantations, to stir in the collective psyche a response that was no doubt first aroused by the high priestess and the medicine man. It is first channeled by every new generation toward Teacher, but it will also engulf the Preacher and the Scoutmaster; (even the Bartender is not totally immune to it).

The proof that this is an instinctive and not a learned response is that it is at its most virulent in its youngest practitioners—innocent tots between the ages of five and twelve. In fact, it is probable that it exists in its pure form only in prepubescent humans and that apparent manifestations of it in adolescents and adults are due to habituation or arrested development.

The teacher image is obviously not just a modified form of the familiar parental one. The teacher role is primarily aphysiological, and in this it bears no relation to the role of parents. Parents bleed, sweat, and sigh, and they may even belch or blow their noses discreetly without inducing trauma in their offspring. But children have been known to go into a state of shock at their first sight of a teacher eating. I have seen stunned disillusionment in the eyes of pupils who caught me in the supermarket as their gaze went from my mundane purchases to me, absorbing the full horror of the implications.

The force of those infantile expectations results in a kind of brainwashing of their object, and only the most iron-willed of elementary teachers can hold out against it. Before long they will find themselves almost incapable of any unteacherly conduct, even when they are alone and in the privacy of their boudoirs. (That is, of course, the explanation of the low marriage rate among elementary teachers.)

College professors are far from free from the effects of the carry-over of this process, though they are more inclined to resist it. Still, it is a rare teacher of any kind who can hope to be completely successful in the attempt, and many of them wind up in a worse condition than if they had surrendered without a fight. Such gestures as wearing T-shirts, drinking beer, and using four-letter words will not conceal an underlying schoolmasterly soul.

At the end of five years, I had irreversibly become a teacher, but I had accomplished nothing toward my long-range goal of getting out of the Ozarks and learning enough about the world to write. My salary had been reduced every year, as the Depression hung on, and I had had to borrow money every summer to continue work on a degree. I was then getting sixty-five dollars a month, for nine months, and at the end of every school year I still owed some of the money I had borrowed the previous summer. I had a hundred and fifty college hours, thirty more than were required for a degree, but many of them were in French and Spanish and didn't count, and I lacked two required elementary education courses. So, when I saw an ad in the Kansas City *Star* for traveling magazine agents, I borrowed the money to go to Kansas City, and was taken on.

After I had come back to Springfield and had started getting some things published, my college English professor and I became friends.

She asked me once why I hadn't become an English teacher, and I reminded her of our fateful conference. I told her that I had always admired her for having seen through me, in spite of my great disappointment at the time.

"You were right," I said. "I could never have put up with the chore of grading composition papers. It was better to get as far away from my field as I could, if I was going to teach at all."

She didn't agree. She insisted that she had only meant to spur me on—that she had known that the classwork was too easy for me and was only trying to inspire me to greater efforts. She said she had expected me back and had wondered why I had switched majors.

That may have been true. But I really think she had forgotten the episode. At any rate, I didn't share her regret for the outcome for very long. On the contrary, I've often mentally expressed my gratitude to her for rescuing me from permanent schoolmarmery by having sensed intuitively, as I thought, that I wasn't cut out for it.

6

It was through having to learn to sell magazine sub-
scriptions to strange men in strange cities, and to live *en
famille* with a very diversified crew of strange girls, that
I eventually rejoined the human race—which I had begun
to slip away from shortly after I had started reading
books. Detached as I had been about my various roles up
to then, and superficial as I had felt them to be, they had
nevertheless had their effect on my external self.

In grade school I was already beginning to identify
with Prudence and her friends, and by the time I was in
high school I had molded myself into the teachers' idea
of the model all-around girl. In fact, I was nominated
by a faculty committee for the title of "Best All-Around
Girl" in my senior year—to my own immense embarrassment. I knew by then that I had an image that was too
prudish, bookish, and ethereal to win a student election
for the honor, and that, besides my social status, disqualified me. I lost resoundingly.

The impression I made by my angelic conduct in high
school was enhanced by my appearance. I was tall and
thin and had large clear blue eyes, very fine pale blond

hair (which I wore straight, with bangs) and a translucent, ivory complexion. I matured late, and all through high school I had a straight-up-and-down childish figure, and I wore childish clothes—prim blouses and skirts, flat heels, and no make-up.

Although I had felt sexual stirrings early, and had been constantly in and out of love ever since I was eleven, I had sternly repressed all such feelings after I left Chitwood, as unsuitable to my role as earnest student and mother's helper. Besides, the high school boys who attracted me were put off by my unabashed intellectuality in the classroom, not to mention my impossible social position, and the two or three who did become friends with me, in spite of my handicaps, were themselves sexless eggheads—or so they struck me.

My aim then, anyway, had been to put sex—that working-class preoccupation—out of my life, at least temporarily, and I almost succeeded. This was easy during the first couple of years, when I was able to retain the illusion that total sexual purity was the rule among adolescents in the aseptic world I was living on the fringes of, and when I certainly had no doubts that this was what their elders expected of them. Then I had the first of two or three encounters with middle-class adolescent lust that proved to be as enlightening about that milieu as my first intimation of the breadth of the middle-class vocabulary had been.

The first of these was on a blind date, arranged for me by Mary Anne Calbert, the democratic neighbor of my employers. I knew the boys involved only casually —they were seniors and Mary Anne and I were juniors— but their fathers were Rotary and Country Club associates of the Hortons, with prominent names, and I expected a very proper evening. I wasn't even suspicious when they headed for Reding's Mill, a riverbank park five miles out of town, where I had been on school picnics, and my date confided to me that Mary Anne had told him I was a fooler—a real down-to-earth kid, who knew the score, in spite of my holier-than-thou manner.

On the way out, I must have fanned the boy's hopes. Mary Anne and I were practicing Alfalfa intermittently, and as we went by a downtown movie, I saw on the marquee, "The Marx Brothers in Duck Soup" and began, "The Marlfarx Brulfuthers in . . ." Then Mary Anne and I burst into peals of giggling, in which the boys joined us after figuring out the horrendous conclusion of the transformed title.

After we got to the park, though, I soon saw that my attempts at animated conversation were beginning to fall flat, and I caught on when Mary Anne and her date got out of the car, took a blanket from the back seat, and strolled up the riverbank. My date immediately moved over and began what I was to learn later (by contrast) were some quite perfunctory amorous advances. I demurred, and, when he persisted, I got out of the car, walked over and sat on a bench by a picnic table. After a while he joined me there and announced that he had made up his mind to kiss me, and that he wouldn't take me home until he had. I then informed him that I was saving my lips for the man I loved, and that if he was so depraved that he could not respect such a resolution, I would walk home rather than relent. That gave him due pause, I thought. At any rate, he immediately desisted and went back and sat in the car. I remained haughtily on the bench, and was on the point of deciding I was going to have to carry out my threat—reluctant as I was to start walking—when the other couple reappeared, and my date yelled at me to come and get in the car.

We were all subdued on the way home. Mary Anne and her date were continuing to neck in the back seat, I supposed—though I didn't look around to see. My date concentrated stonily on his driving.

I went around all the next day with the reassuring conviction that I had handled a difficult situation in an irreproachable manner. Then that evening, as Mrs. Horton and I were getting dinner in the kitchen, she gave me one of her merry looks and said tauntingly, "So you're saving your lips for the man you love!" Gay laughter. "Oh, that's absolutely priceless! I imagine that's the first time Tommy Montgomery ever heard that one. I don't suppose he ever read a book."

I said nothing. I was too overcome by the implications of what I had heard.

"Tommy thought it was hilarious," Mrs. Horton continued, "and so did his parents. Madge told us about it today at the bridge club. Marie Latimer had just been telling us a good one. The other day she was getting the cleaning ready to go out and found a package of safes in Johnny's pocket. When she called him on it that evening, he said, 'But mother, you have to protect a nice girl.' All the girls said this just proved what high school girls are like these days, and, of course Madge Montgomery had to tell her little story. Were you really going to walk home rather than let your lips be sullied?"

I said, "Yes ma'am," and went on peeling potatoes, embarrassment at my own naïveté, though I did feel that too, being among the minor emotions that were assailing me. Uppermost in my mind were the shocking realization that I had finally relinquished all claims to privacy, and the sense of an urgent need to flee while there was still time. I had already had unsettling intimations that my peculiar position as a poor kid who was competing scholastically with the rich kids was making me disgustingly conspicuous. There was, for example, the overprivileged neighbor girl who told me she prayed nightly that I'd go back to wherever I came from because she got so sick of her parents pointing to me as someone she should be able to do at least one tenth as well as, considering. Then there was the vote by the committee-of-the-whole of the Women of Rotary to take me on as the recipient of their shoe-fund charity, and the consequent blow to philanthropy when I turned them down, after one mortifying shopping excursion in the company of a Rotary Ann. It wasn't just that I detested letting every shoe store manager in town know that I was accepting charity. I also had feet that were embarrassingly big and hard to fit in anything that was at all stylish. The Rotary Ann was more interested in durability than in style and she finally foisted a pair of sensible shoes, for which my loathing must have been obvious, off on me. I never wore them, and I never heard from the Rotary Women again—but I feared I might.

Even after such intimations of the publicness of my role, however, I was still stunned that my views on necking could have been the topic of conversation at a high-society gathering and that these views were ridiculed rather than supported. I found the knowledge both enlightening and threatening. Apparently these exalted beings did expect everyone to engage in a certain amount of illicit sex, after all, and, obviously, my own sexual conduct—whether right or wrong—was likely to become common knowledge. I was struck at that moment by the

full extent of the sacrifice I had made for the sake of becoming educated, and I bitterly regretted it. I thought
seriously of abandoning the potatoes in mid-peel, packing
my things—leaving the Rotary shoes in the middle of my
room—and hitchhiking to Newton County, where my family had moved. Two things stopped me. In the first place,
the gesture would have been lost on Mrs. Horton and her
friends—I could imagine her saying, "She got peeved and
ran off because I teased her about her love life." In the
second place, and of more importance, I had already
gone too far to think of retreating. I no longer belonged in
Newton County. I resolved, instead, to avoid any future
personal entanglements and to continue to act the model
student-cum-mother's-helper for just as long as I had to.

What this sort of life did to me, by the end of the next
school year when I had completed a semester at the Baptist junior college, was—among other things—to make me
almost unemployable. I could write poetry, parse sentences, do geometry and algebra problems, read Latin,
and speak French, and I could cook and keep house. But
I had acquired a prim look and a high-toned manner of
speech that caused cafeteria managers and factory fore-
men to back off from me instinctively. Some of my fellow
college students in Springfield worked as waitresses or
factory hands, but I was stuck with the housekeeping routine and saw no immediate way out but schoolteaching,
so I hurried to get the required college hours as fast as
I could.

And then I found that teaching school was only exac-
erbating my image problem. After five years of that, I
discovered that I bore even more strongly defined stigmata, and moved in a world even farther removed from
the world of reality.

So the ad in the Kansas City *Star*—"H.S. grads, over 21, free to travel South and New England, expenses guaranteed"—sounded like the perfect way out to me, and I took the money I had borrowed for summer school, went to Kansas City, checked in at the best hotel, and went to apply for the job. I hadn't intended to tell the crew manager I was a schoolteacher, but he guessed it right away and told me I wouldn't do. "In the first place," he said, "we've found that schoolteachers don't like this work, and, in the second place, they can't sell."

He said he had to guarantee fare home for any prospects he fired and he didn't think enough of my chances to risk the expense. In my desperation, I told him that I had two hundred dollars in travelers' checks which I would give him to hold for my return fare and to help pay for my expenses if I didn't earn enough.

He agreed to that arrangement, still reluctantly, and only on a trial basis. He explained that the car space I would occupy was valuable, and that, besides, a nonproducer was bad for the morale of the rest of the crew, the expense aside.

He was interviewing me in the lobby of the second-rate hotel that had been listed in the want ad, and he told me that the crew would be working in Kansas City for one more day, and that I should report to his room there the next morning to start training.

At eight o'clock the next morning, when I got to the door with the number on it he had given me, I heard loud voices on the other side.

"You're crazy! Meshugah!" screamed a youngish female voice. "I got my goddam quota. You promised me! 'Get forty today, Carol, and we'll go shopping tomorrow.' I got fifty. Fifty stinkin' orders in one day, and today I'm supposed to take a damn dumb schoolteacher out and train her! Well, up your bucket, bud! I quit. Give me my money."

"Now, listen, Carol. I got two prospects on that ad, and you know we practically have one empty car. I need somebody that can show this kid some business till we get her out of town, where she'll have to learn to produce. You can do it in a couple of hours, then bring her in, and we'll *go* shopping."

"Give me my money, you cheat! You dirty crook! I know why you don't pay me. You can't! You haven't got the hotel bill."

"All right, that's enough, you little bitch! Get to your room." The door in front of me was thrown open and a small plumpish brunette with tousled short hair and blazing brown eyes flashed past me. Mr. Anderson grabbed the doorknob and yelled after her, "And pack! Be ready to check out of here in half an hour, or I'll have you thrown out. You'll get your lousy money."

"Oh, good morning, Miss Reed," he said to me, unperturbedly. "Come in. Have a chair. I'll be with you in a moment."

There were six or eight other girls in the room, seated on the bed, on chairs, on a sofa—all attractive and well-dressed and all looking calm to the point of boredom. Mr. Anderson handed a set of car keys to one of them, a slim refined-looking brunette, who was wearing a white sharkskin suit, a broad-brimmed hat, and white gloves. "Take the Buick, Miss Wilson," he said, "and get these girls out on territory. Call me at noon."

Then he said to me, "Let's you and I go down and have some coffee. Miss Palenik's gone to her room to fix her face. She'll be down in a little while. I imagine this is the last we'll see of our other new girl, so we're going to have plenty of space for you after all. You might as well see what Jawjia is like, anyway."

Mr. Anderson ordered breakfast and I was nervously drinking my cup of coffee and telling him about my previous exodus from the Ozarks—to the Chicago World's Fair—when Miss Palenik appeared. "Well, our prima donna arrives," Mr. Anderson said. "And ten to one she hasn't had breakfast. Join us, Miss Palenik. I'm buying."

"Cram it," said Miss Palenik. "Let's get going."

"Well sit down, anyway, and try to act like a lady. Though I know it'll be a strain. This is Miss Reed. Miss Reed is a schoolteacher, from the Ozarks, and she's not used to little New Jersey Polacks. She won't understand. She might think you really mean all those unkind things you say to me."

The girl sat down, but continued to ignore me. "Miss Palenik is really a very nice girl," Mr. Anderson said to me. "And she loves the magazine business. I keep telling her she ought to be back in Paterson with her husband, but I can't get rid of her. She's going to show you this morning how easy it is."

We three went in a new De Soto to a race track outside the city where Miss Palenik said she had some callbacks. She had been silent on the way out, and when we got out of the car, she said, "Okay, kid. Follow me and keep your mouth shut. They're running some gyp races here this afternoon and there are some owners and trainers I've got to see fast, before the races start."

Suddenly all smiling vivacity, Carol introduced herself and me to the first prospect she cornered and told him that she needed only a few more points to win an all-expense trip to the New York World's Fair, and that Tom

Pendergast was backing her—"and I guess you know what *that* means." He said he did, and then she showed him the stubs from a pile of other orders, mentioning a dozen prominent politicians and officeholders, and the man said he'd take two. She met with similar success in all her other interviews, collecting five or ten dollars each for various magazines from six or eight men, and went back to the car triumphant.

"Well, I got 'em, Simon Legree," she said.

"I knew you would, baby," Mr. Anderson said. "So now go buy yourself a whole new outfit. Where do you want to go? I. Magnin's?"

"Take me to the courthouse," she said. "I got some real hot leads there. Those guys told me that no protégée of Tom Pendergast's should pass up all those judges and sheriff's deputies. I've been using the sheriff's name all over the place, and I'd better see him just to keep myself honest."

We did go through the courthouse, and the officeholders were just as easy as the horse trainers. I finally began to suspect that most of them didn't know or care whether or not Miss Palenik had ever so much as set eyes on the redoubtable Tom Pendergast, the political boss, and finally one salty old judge said as much.

After she laughingly countered his questions about what Tom Pendergast looked like, when and where she had last seen him, etc., he said, "You're a horrible little fraud, Miss Palenik, but it's an education to watch you work. Give me a couple more of those things."

We left Kansas City that afternoon and got into a hotel in Little Rock, Arkansas, that night. The next morning Miss Wilson took me to a street in a small business district, made a couple of calls with me, got one order for a cheap magazine, and sent me forth on my own, with instructions to report to Mr. Anderson at the hotel at noon. Everybody I talked to turned me down flat and, when I reported to Mr. Anderson at noon, I gave him one despairing look, burst into tears, and wailed, "I can't do it." He bought my lunch, patiently went over my spiel with me, made me promise to give it a week, then took me back to my uninspiring-looking territory.

The very first man I talked to that afternoon bought a two-years' subscription to *House Beautiful*. It was the only order I got that day, but I had the feel of it and, by late summer when we finally got to New England, I was giving Miss Palenik competition, and was making, above my expenses, as much in a week as I had made in a month teaching school.

Mr. Anderson knew that I had signed a contract to teach the next year and, as September approached, he began trying to persuade me to stay. He offered to assign me a car of my own, with a crew on which I could make a percentage, and to give me my choice of territory. I was still uncertain that I could ever be anything but a schoolteacher, but I wrote and asked for a year's leave of absence, which I was granted. By the time that year was up, I was confident of my ability to sell and to manage people and I knew that I had escaped forever from the confines of the classroom and the kitchen, which seemed equally unappealing to me at the time—and ever since, for that matter.

The knowledge that I had a skill that made me independent in a society such as ours was greatly liberating to me. I didn't have much respect for the job I was doing, but at least, I thought, I was doing no harm, and there were features of the specific job that I especially liked. I loved the freedom of constant travel—the lack of ties—the sense of evading all social obligations. The very atmosphere of a strange city was exhilarating to me. The names of streets and buildings would become familiar to me from the reminiscings of the other girls before I had seen them, and it gave me a romantic thrill to be lost among their denizens later in the guise of one of their number. I found that sort of relationship with places much more satisfying than mere sight-seeing, which never interested me. It gave me pleasure to be purposefully using Grand Central Terminal and the Pennsylvania Station, Park Avenue and the Chrysler Building, Peachtree Street in Atlanta, Grantiot and Woodward avenues and the Penobscott Building in Detroit, Market Street in San Francisco, Milk Street in Boston, and Hollywood and Vine in Los Angeles.

I also faced the fact that what I was doing was for me the next best thing to suicide, which had begun to strike me as the sane and logical solution to everything in my early adolescence. I felt no responsibilities, no obligations, and few restraints. The other girls in the group were gay and friendly, and we shared one short-range goal—to get our quota for the day.

I had little trouble with that, after the first month or two. Miss Palenik's demonstration of the power of name-dropping was not lost on me, and I improved on the method by carefully calculating which were the most efficacious names to drop where. By working this out and acting on it, I eventually learned a great deal about the hierarchy of American business. Railroad men—even railroad presidents—are impressed by the names of important shippers; steel-company executives are impressed by the names of railroad presidents and railroad purchasing agents, and so on. To lessen the tension that having to fake an acquaintance with the bearers of the names caused me, I soon began actually seeing them first, and, as proof for the next ones, I had them sign a small autograph book that I carried around in my purse.

My natural curiosity, gregariousness, and gift for small talk, which I had had to repress in all my other roles except in my brief and intermittent one as a college student, proved very useful to me in my peddler role. As soon as the tycoons had ceased to awe me, I was usually able to open a conversation with them easily, though occasionally an impromptu opening would bomb. For example, the first man I went to see on my first morning in Philadelphia was a popular Pennsylvania Railroad official. When I got on the elevator in the station to go to his office, I noticed that the elevator operator, a young Negro in a smart uniform, had a large, remarkable waxed mustache—the first one I had ever seen. My first words to my prospect, when he rose to greet me and I had introduced myself, were, "I just saw an admirer of yours on the elevator." The official was wearing an imposing replica of the elevator boy's mustache.

Naturally he was eager to know more. I said, "It was the operator. I guess you know he's a fan of yours."

He said, "No. What did he say?"

"I just gathered that he admires your appearance," I told him, and hastily went on to my spiel with the autograph book.

Before the day was over, I learned why my remark had fallen flat. Half of the men I called on, and one out of every three men on the streets of Philadelphia had their faces adorned with Daliesque mustaches. I had misinterpreted what was only a local custom.

Then, at a small elegant plant in Pittsburgh, the manager, a handsome and haughty young man, came out to
greet me, then sent me on back to his beautifully appointed office while he stopped to talk to someone else.
After some time, I picked up a photo on his desk and ex-
amined it. It was of a woman in riding clothes standing
by a horse. The woman looked past middle age and
had an unusually ugly face and a lumpy figure. I was re-
flecting on the incongruity of her appearance with the
rest of the décor as I set the photo back on the desk,
when I looked up and saw my prospect. He was regarding me with an expression that suggested he had read my
thoughts, and I was completely disconcerted.

"Your mother?" I asked, knowing as soon as the words
were out that I had a fifty-fifty chance of having committed a fatal error.

"That's my wife," he said belligerently.

By that time I was completely undone, but he stood
there as if challenging me to redeem myself, and the
best I could do, in the split second I had was, "It's a beautiful horse!"

Most of the men I was calling on by that time felt
some constraint as to what they could say to me. They
knew or believed that I had seen some of their friends
and competitors and would see others, and this enforced
on them a certain circumspection.

The horsewoman's husband, however, I had called on
cold, so he felt free to say what he wanted to. What he
said was, "Get out!" This seemed so exactly the right thing
to me that I felt like applauding him. I hastened to
obey.

Whether I tackled them with or without leads, I was
finding that the men in the so-called heavy industries

were the most tractable. Steel, coal, oil, railroad, and steamship-company executives were usually genial types who enjoyed talking with someone so unlike their usual run of daily callers, and they could therefore be sold. Among railroad officials—the field in which I was specializing—the degree of tractability depended on what department the prospect was in. Men in the passenger-traffic and personal-claims departments were as impervious to charm and cajolery, and as likely to be waspish and picayune, as men in the professions; those in the freight-traffic and freight-claims departments were more like the men in the mechanical and operating departments. My first deduction from this was that a prospect's susceptibility was affected by whether or not he had to deal with as many women as men in his daily job; that to those who did, I probably looked like just another problem, even at first sight.

But, after more prolonged observation of the personalities of professional men, I learned that lawyers, who also deal with both sexes, were salable, while doctors, dentists, and professors usually were not. So my final verdict was that the occupational differences in the tractability of prospects depended on their professional posture toward the people they dealt with in their daily work. Lawyers were the shrewdest, as could be expected. And doctors, dentists, and professors were the most gullible—if you could ever get their ear, but that was hard to do. On their jobs they are used to dealing with captive audiences, people to whom they are always in a superior position, so they are not accustomed to having to persuade anybody, or to permitting themselves to be persuaded. They go on the assumption that they already know before you open your mouth exactly what they want and what they believe and they are determined that nothing you can say will change their minds. That is a point of pride with all three groups. I would guess, from wide experience with doctors, dentists, and professors from coast to coast, that there are few men in any of the three professions who have admitted a new thought into their heads since they began practicing their professions.

Of the three professions, I found dentists the most inflexibly know-it-all and overbearing; and once, when I was in Chicago and had the afternoon off to get a small, expensive dental job done, I planned a nasty revenge on the whole profession. I went into a large building full of dentists' offices and deliberately approached one after another of them in a manner that I knew would bring out the worst in them. To do this I only had to revert mentally to my first few weeks in the magazine business when nearly every man I tried to talk to would say, after my first few words, "Whatever you're selling, I don't want any," or the equivalent. As soon as I was able to figure out exactly what it was about my manner and tone of voice that could make even a dentist feel instantly safe in assuming that I was not, say, an Evanston coed with a dental problem, and as soon as I was able to apply a little Method-acting technique to overcome that handicap, I was able to at least get into my sales talk, even with dentists.

My ear (and tongue) for language served me well in my impersonations of an Evanston coed who might have a toothache, or an Atlanta-suburban newlywed looking for a diaphragm, or a Westchester Junior Leaguer contemplating divorce. Of course I never *said* I was any of those things. I prided myself on getting by without openly lying. But I knew that, if there was something so obvious about the look and manner of a magazine agent that even a dentist could spot one immediately, there had to be something about these other various types that set *them* apart, too, and that all I had to do to alter my own image was to think myself into being one or the other of them temporarily.

The Method technique was superfluous with the railroad and railway-supply men I eventually got set with, though it helped me in getting by their chief clerks and secretaries. But, if I was stuck in a town where I had run out of prospects in those lines and had to start canvassing cold, I always used it—taking first the lawyers, then the doctors, then the college professors, if there was a college in the town, and, last, the dentists.

On my retaliatory tour of those dentists' offices in Chicago that day, I kept my Evanston coed manner toward the dentists' office girls, and then I reverted to my amateur-book-agent manner as soon as I had the dentist cornered.

I would blurt in an anxious singsong: "Dr. Blank, I'm calling on some of your associates in the building this morning, and Dr. So-and-So next door said I shouldn't miss you?" (Voice raised at the end.)

The typical dentist would come back with, "All right, sister, what are you selling?"

I would go on, "I'm not exactly selling anything, Doctor, but I have something here I'd like to show you, if I could have just a moment of your time."

Dentist: "I'm too busy to put up with any spiel now. You people would do better if you'd just come right out and say what you want than to beat around the bush."

At that point I would open my mouth, point at a back

molar, and deliver my punch line: "Well, Doctor, I need a gold crown on this tooth right here, and four fillings. But I certainly don't want to keep you from more important things. Good day!"

I ran through about a dozen dentists in an hour with that approach, enjoying every minute of it. A few of my victims were left speechless, but most of them tried to rectify things by telling me they had thought I was a magazine agent and how they felt about those. Then I would tell them I was one and what I thought about dentists, and then go into an explanation of why I was playing my little game. Naturally I remained unmoved by subsequent apologies.

Finally I ran into a nice young man who was willing to hear my story, whatever it might be, and, when he learned that it was dental work I was after, his pleased surprise was most gratifying. I paid him fifty dollars for his work and never did tell him what my occupation was. He did a good job; I still have the gold crown, and the fillings—and, more important, the teeth.

I was gradually becoming adept at judging the flexibility of all kinds of men almost on sight, and the most profitable thing I learned was that those who acted the most unapproachable to begin were likely to turn out to be the freest spenders in the end; painful experience had taught them that once they let the bars down they were lost, so they had adopted an impregnable façade in self-defense. On the other hand, those who were the most gracious about receiving a salesman and inviting him to spin out his full sales pitch were usually the sort who did so because they were so confident of their own invulnerability.

Then I ran into a steel-company representative in Chicago who was a maddening combination of the two types. A huge, shy, rugged-looking bachelor (I could infallibly guess any man's marital and familial status by then), the steel man was, by turns, coldly gruff and graciously receptive until, after half an hour or so of his blowing hot and cold, I decided to give up. I stood up and said icily, "Mr. Hamilton, I don't think you know what you want. For some reason, it seems to amuse you to see me wasting my time." I intended to stalk haughtily out of the room, but I had gone only a few steps when I burst out bawling.

He ordered me to come back and sit down, but I declined, until he pointed out, in gentler tones, that I couldn't go out in the street in the condition I was in. After I had sat down, still sniffing and unmollified, he said, "Let me see that thing again."

"No. I don't want you to buy anything you don't want. I'm not that bad off," I said peevishly.

"But I do want a couple," he insisted. "I was just going to tell you when you decided to pull that act."

I pushed my list across the desk to him, still feeling offended and a little suspicious of his intentions. When he had the list in his hands, he switched again, "And don't think that bawling act had any effect on me," he said. "I detest women that think they can get their way by turning on the tears."

I must have looked a little skeptical, or perhaps he realized that his protestations were unconvincing. "The fact is," he went on, "that when you stood up there to leave you reminded me of my sister. You looked just like her. And that reminded me that I was going to send her some magazines. What's this *Ladies' Home Journal*?"

He completed his order, selecting four magazines, and, as he was making out the check, he warned me sternly, "I hope this doesn't give you the idea the sob stuff is going to help you make any more sales. That's an old trick, and it won't ever get you anywhere. It's just lucky for you in this case that you happened to remind me of my sister."

While I was putting my order book away, he got up and put on his coat and hat, then he mutely accompanied me to the elevator and rode down with me, all without a word. I began to wonder what I was getting into, and decided that, in any case, it was probably prudent to maintain my injured air. When we got out in the lobby, he spoke his first words to me since he had grumblingly given me the check.

"Do you smoke?" he asked me enigmatically. I said yes; he asked me what brand; then stopped at the magazine stand, bought a package of the brand I mentioned, and thrust it at me. When we got outside the building, he asked, "Have you had lunch?"

I thought, "Oh, no! Lord spare me from sitting through lunch with this type."

He must have guessed the reason for my hesitation. "I always eat early myself," he said. "But I kept you so long, you probably haven't eaten. If you haven't, you go right over there, see?" He pointed down the street. "They have good wholesome food and it's not expensive." Then he soberly stuck out his large paw to shake hands and said good-by, still without smiling, and then he rushed back into the building.

I recall other odd encounters that were more satisfying if less profitable—and less touching. Two of the most absurd were, naturally enough, in Los Angeles. One of these

involved a Santa Fe railroad official who yelled, the minute I walked into his office, "You were in here just three
weeks ago, and I told you I don't want any magazines.
Now here you are again."

I had slipped up; I had forgotten his name, when somebody gave it to me again, but as soon as I saw his face I
knew that I had seen him before and that he was one of
those that I usually marked "n.g." upon first meeting and
carefully avoided thereafter.

I said, "It was inadvertent, I assure you."

"You people never give up, do you?" he persisted. "You
get a name on your list, and you just keep after us. You
think you'll wear us down. But this is one time you're
mistaken."

I said, "Believe me, Mr. Schultz, I'd forgotten you completely. If I hadn't, I certainly wouldn't be here. You're
practically accusing me of being a masochist."

He froze and eyed me suspiciously, "What do you
mean?" he demanded.

I said, "A goddam hog for punishment, that's what!"
and exited.

The other Los Angeles fiasco was with an oil-company
president, whose name had been given me by another
executive who said that he had lost quite a bit of money
at poker to my prospect the night before.

Of course I used that bit of information in my intro-
ductory gambit. But it must have been the prospect who
had lost. At any rate, the reference to the poker game
seemed to irritate him alarmingly. He eyed me hostilely
and said, "All right, let's get down to business. What do
you want?"

I saw that I had been fatally misled, and stood up to
leave. "Nothing," I said. "I did have a minor matter I was

going to take up with you, but after your hostile reception I've changed my mind."

"I know what you want," he said. "You're selling something. You want me to buy some tickets, or some magazines, or something. So get on with it. I've got a right to know what it is." By this time his face was flushed and his eyes were blazing.

I said, "No, I don't want to discuss it. With the mood you're in this morning, I'd be wasting my breath."

"I'm *not* in any mood this morning!" he shouted. "I mean my mood has nothing to do with it!"

I said, "Perhaps not. Maybe you're like this all the time. But that seems hard to believe. It would wreck your circulatory system."

"I'll find out," he said, and he then rang furiously for his secretary.

During all this exchange I had been standing near the door, poised to leave. I stepped back and smiled at the secretary as she rushed in, looking distraught.

"Get me Don Lambert on the phone," he ordered her.

I expected a deflating anticlimax momentarily, of course, but dignity forbade my departure at this point, so I stood my ground, looking, I hoped, smilingly inscrutable.

Luck was with me, however. Mr. Lambert, the man who had sent me there, was out.

When he learned this, my ex-prospect did almost reach the explosion point.

"I insist that you tell me what you came in here for," he yelled. Then he assumed a crafty look. "I know what I'll do, I'll call the police."

"Go ahead," I said. "Call them. They'll know that I'm exercising my constitutional rights."

That expression just flew into my head. I didn't think it meant much. But it was the first thing I had said that seemed to give my adversary pause. He cooled off visibly. So I pursued it. "The Constitution of the United States gives its citizens freedom of speech. *And* freedom not to speak," I said sententiously, "and I'm standing on my rights."

At that the man looked utterly whipped, and I went out, slamming the door behind me.

7

IN A MAN'S WORLD

I have observed a few dogs that seem to be under the delusion that they are people, and I fear that for most of my life I have been afflicted by a similar delusion. Intellectually, I seem to have harbored an unconscious conviction that I am a man. Not that I have ever had any conspicuous masculine characteristics. Emotionally, I have always had all the typically feminine weaknesses and none of the typically masculine strengths, in spite of all my efforts to improve in that regard. And neither I nor anyone else—so far as I know—has ever had any reason to suspect that my intellectual illusion has ever affected my sexual orientation. But repeated jarring reminders, doubly wounding to my tender female psyche, that my mentality is also female, and therefore has its narrowly proscribed place, have not driven that truth home.

It's surprising that there are not more girls with this intellectual delusion: the schools foster it relentlessly. Public educational systems and coeducational colleges are geared to train the brightest students to be "leaders," without making any provision for that half or more of the academically superior contingent of the student body which is precluded by nature from ever filling the leadership role. Most girls seem to accept this debarment by the time they get through college, but those of us who have been encouraged to think of ourselves as writers take longer, and some of us never totally perceive the truth.

It was Miss Dora Heald, my fifth-grade teacher in Chitwood, who first caused me to cast myself in the writer's role. As a teacher in an urban school system, Miss Heald was the first teacher I had had who had gone beyond the eighth grade and who knew something about pedagogical techniques. She discovered right away that I knew no arithmetic, and she used the last half of my study periods for the first couple of weeks I was in her room to teach me the combinations upside down and backward. (From then on, I lacked even the saving feminine grace of being weak in mathematics.) After I had my combinations down perfectly, I would use my free time to peruse Miss Heald's scrapbooks. She had about a dozen of them, filled mostly with clippings from the rotogravure sections of Sunday newspapers. Those were for me the forerunner of educational television, and I went through them all at least twice, bringing myself up to date on what I had missed by not reading the newspapers as they came out during the previous five years or so of my literate life. I assumed then that Miss Heald, who impressed me as being not only selfless, but sexless and emotionless, spent all of her out-of-school time in quest of newspaper material that would be painlessly instructive to nine-year-olds, but that did not strike me then as an odd avocation.

It was under Miss Heald's tutelage that I wrote my first poems and the only fiction I ever remember writing. She thought my poems were good because they all had perfect rhyme and meter, and one of them did place in a city-wide contest. But the effect that one of my short stories had on her gave me a much more stunning sense of accomplishment. The story was a first-person account of a narrow escape on a railroad trestle, in the teeth of an approaching Joplin-and-Pittsburg interurban streetcar, and I feared it was too lurid even to be a good story, but Miss Heald filled me with a bemused confidence in my own creative talents by asking me if the story was true. I wrote a few more stories that year which Miss Heald thought sounded true, but by the next year I decided that I had been misled by the fact that Miss Heald was merely unusually gullible, no doubt from having confined her reading to the Sunday supplements. I have never since been able to write even the truth in fictional form so that it sounded true, even to me. I once got an invitation from a *New Yorker* magazine fiction editor who had read an article of mine to submit such a story; and, though the invitation seemed to me at the time to be almost the highest possible accolade—second only to having a story published in the *New Yorker*—I was never able to bring myself to go beyond the first page. By then, the phoniness of what I had written was always so patent that I couldn't bring myself to go on.

I ceased being a poet during my first year in college. It was then that I discovered that, though I no longer had gushes of inspiration, I could still turn out poems that struck everybody else as just as good as those I had written at the behest of the Muse, if not better. That disillusioning realization doused my poetic fire forever.

Ever since I had started writing for the high school paper, I had regarded myself primarily as a critic, essayist, and wit anyway, and fancied that in my better things I saw touches of Swift, Shaw, Mencken, or some lesser writer in that genre, but only of the male ones. Like members of any oppressed group, I have always been inclined to accept the view of the dominant group as to the worth of my own. In fact, I can't think of anything that would strike me as less likely to be worth reading, if I had to judge it only by the author's sex and point of origin, than an idea piece by a woman from Southwest Missouri, unless it was one by a woman from Kansas.

Still, I always feel inexplicably rebuffed when my own pieces are returned to me by Eastern editors with vague excuses and apologies, the sum of which is usually: "The editors here all find your article very amusing and perceptive, but we feel that your subject is too special to appeal to a general audience." I usually accept that explanation as honest, but more than once the same editors have published articles soon afterward on the same "too-special" subject—written by males. However, I rarely suspect even conscious discrimination in such cases, and I certainly never suspect anything worse, as any man in that position would be justified in doing. After the initial shock, I always manage to put myself in the editor's shoes and see my rejected manuscript as he must have seen it —as a presumptuous offering by some aggressive female from the lumpen Middle West.

In one illuminating case I happened to see a certain editor one summer just a year after he had suggested I wait that long to complete a piece he had prematurely assigned to me, and for which I had done many hours of research and preliminary work. At our second encounter, instead of reminding me that the time was ripe, he asked me in all innocence and friendliness to give him my opinion of a piece on my topic (by a man) which was coming out in the next issue of his magazine. It was obviously inconceivable to that editor that any woman would place anything she might write in the same category as something written by a man, or that she would consider herself in competition with any male writer. It would have occurred to him that I had justifiable cause for feeling offense only if he had used something else—on any topic —by some other Middle Western woman at that time. All canine actors are in the same category, and you wouldn't want two on the same bill, but a canine comic and a human comic are not considered to be in competition, and neither is likely to suspect the other of stealing his stuff.

Dorothy M. Sayers, the British creator of Lord Peter Wimsey, wrote about her frustrating experiences with editors of journals of opinion. A theologian as well as a detective-story writer, Miss Sayers kept being puzzled by the complimentary rejection letters she was getting from those editors and tried to pin them down. Driven to the wall, one of them finally informed her: "The public do not like to be admonished by a woman."

This is especially true of the American public. There are no American counterparts of Barbara Ward (British) or Hannah Arendt (German) or Simone de Beauvoir (French)—women whose opinions on whatever subject they choose to write about are given some weight by the male experts in their fields, and whose styles and personalities are disregarded. Once I thought for a moment recently that Joseph Wood Krutch, writing as a drama critic on drama critics, had made a breakthrough in this regard. He cited an opinion of Marion Magid's, but soon referred to her as "he," and a little later, proving that this was not a typographical error, as "Mr. Magid."

An American woman who wants to get her ideas published must first become established for her wit (Jean Kerr), or a sharp tongue—which is itself more amusing than wounding in such an impotent creature—(Mary McCarthy), or both (Dorothy Parker). It is fortunate that the early experiences of intelligent girls who aspire to compete in the intellectual arena serve to equip them for their roles. Unless she has had a very sheltered upbringing, any intelligent girl will inevitably come to view life with the sort of resigned irony that is expressed in literary wit and sarcasm.

More than once I have been taken aback by an editorial opinion that something I have dashed off in the heat of a debate that I felt quite serious about was appealing chiefly because of its "humor." And I continue to be affronted by the editorial stipulations I usually get, along with assignments, that I am to treat the subject, no matter how weighty, with my "well-known light touch."

Repeated squelches of this sort have not, however, entirely persuaded the inner me that I cannot argue the issues seriously in print. I continue to try to match wits mentally with the authors of opinion pieces on current issues as I am reading them, and, obtusely and persistently failing to note the sex of the constellation of authors I choose to refute, I haul out my typewriter to talk back. I can see the resemblance here to a small cocker spaniel I used to have who always yearned to join in the human conversation that was going on around her, and thought she was doing so when she wagged her jaws up and down. Her attempts to participate were funny and endearing, but she was failing to get through.

My self-delusion was enhanced by my early work experience after I got out of school. In college I had learned to suppress the impulse to compete openly with males, but the two schools I taught in later were small, insulated, matriarchal hives, and in the magazine-subscription selling business, production was all that counted. You won individual-agent contests; then your crews won group contests; then your agency turned in the most business, so your sex was conveniently, however reluctantly, disregarded.

It would seem that writing, and especially journalistic writing, would be one of the fields in which one's sex would have the least bearing on one's chances to succeed. That's what I thought when I came back to the Ozarks, with husband and son, ready at last to get started on my chosen career as critic and journalist. It soon became evident that I had been wise not to have attempted that career until I had a financial backlog. Still I have been luckier than most would-be female writers who have started out with no special field and a sketchy education. Or—more important, perhaps—without powerful male backing. Is it only an accident that the most successful American women writers of nonfiction were, at the crucial time, the wives or intimate friends of men who were influential in the literary world? Jean Kerr and Mary McCarthy, for example, were the wives of Walter Kerr and Edmund Wilson, respectively, when they first achieved success. (This does not reflect on the talent of the women, but merely points to a fortuitous concatenation of circumstances, lacking which any woman might find literary recognition more difficult.)

My luckiest break, considering my unlikely base of operations, was that I had chosen to live in the same state with the St. Louis *Post-Dispatch*, a large, liberal, respected newspaper, with some venturesome editors on its staff, who also, fortunately, lacked the Eastern view— accurate or not—of Missouri as an outpost of civilization. They started publishing my book reviews and essays right away, and this was not only gratifying and profitable in itself but provided me with a respectable file to show other editors.

In fact, by establishing my credentials as a writer, my first *Post-Dispatch* pieces helped me even in my own region. Soon a local department store hired me to do a radio program "of interest to women," and then I began writing a regular column for the daily newspaper. I quit that over political differences with the editor and joined the staff of a local magazine. Finally, for want of a man who would do the job, I was hired by the International Typographical Union as editor of a daily tabloid the union published for three years in competition with the established daily, which it had struck. On this job I was put in charge of a small staff of reporters, most of them male journalism-school graduates. They were understandably leery of the relationship at first, but later they all turned down better jobs to stick with the union project till it was closed down, even though it was a little shaky from the first. After that, I went back to the broadcasting station, first as a news writer and then as promotion manager. During all my career in local journalism, I continued to write an opinion column on local issues, never lacking an invitation from some kind of publisher who was willing to pay me some sort of remuneration. By default, I eventually established myself through the columns as the sole independent voice of opposition in our town. The management of the town's monopoly newspaper also owns one of the four radio sta-

tions and half of one of the two television stations. The
rest of that station is owned by the owners of another of
the radio stations, and so on. The chief stockholders and
the board presidents of all the radio and television stations all run other, larger, locally-based businesses and
so must often find it expedient to retain the good-will of
the monopoly newspaper, of possible customers and possible advertisers, and, sometimes, of one another. Most
of them also have to rub elbows in the same country club,
on the chamber of commerce board, in the same luncheon
clubs, and on the Republican finance committee. These
social, business, and political affinities of their top men
have naturally inhibited the editorial policies of our local
public-information media, thus leaving me an open field.

My being a woman, and especially a woman with a
"well-known light touch," has made it possible for me to
say things that other local writers couldn't, and to do so
without making any really implacable enemies (so far as
I know). In fact, the men of the local Establishment often
egg me on, giving me inside dope on one another, knowing that I "protect my sources," but knowing also that I
might turn on them the next time.

Come to think of it, the similarity of my local journalistic role to the court jester's is too close for comfort. Your
gibes at your sovereign are accepted by him as salutary
so long as you keep them funny. Get too serious, though,
and it's off with your head. Still, it's not a bad role for a
thwarted female polemicist, and I recommend it. There
are dozens of middle-sized one-newspaper towns in this
country that could use a gadfly. I suspect that the citizens
of these towns would eagerly read anybody's dissenting
opinions on local—and even national—issues even if those
opinions had to be printed on handbills. As a matter of

fact, most middle-sized towns harbor one or two obscure periodicals that would be all the better for a little spice; and, with it, they won't remain quite so obscure for very long. People whose opinions matter, especially those whom you are needling, cannot resist reading provocative opinions on the issues that concern them. Before long any gadfly worthy of the name will find himself with a distinguished, if small, readership.

And the gadfly may frequently have the gratification of having accomplished something truly worth while. I was editing the ITU daily during the McCarthy era, and I helped to ridicule a very militant American Legion Americanism committee out of existence. (For my part in that, I got a "keep-up-the-good-work" note from the late Bernard DeVoto. Mr. DeVoto may not have been among the greatest critics and philosophers in the world, but one thing the lonely gadfly badly needs occasionally is a little outside encouragement.) After that I helped to needle the local school board into integrating the schools a little earlier than they would otherwise have done. As an editor at that time, I not only wrote editorials on those two issues but ran series of instructive news stories—for which the reporters had to keep badgering the principals. They asked the Legionnaires, who were restricting themselves to battling Communist infiltration of Greene County, how many Communists voted in the last Greene County election, for example. (The answer was three.) And they inquired how Stalin would profit from the Springfield library's keeping an old copy of a book by Howard Fast on its shelves. (I can't remember the answer to that one.)

In the end, the Americanism committee was given the *coup de grâce* by the established daily, with which it had gotten into an irrelevant tiff. In its monthly publication, the committee had alleged that the daily was "slanting" its headlines on the McCarthy stories, and the editor of the daily demanded that the Legion disown the committee and withdraw financial support for its publication, on pain of losing the daily's support for its other activities.

In this altercation, I found myself unexpectedly on the side of the Americanism Committee. I agreed that the daily's headlines *were* slanted against McCarthy—even though not so much as I might have slanted them—and I insisted that the Legion as a whole should not be allowed to get by with disavowing the Committee for the piddling reason that it needed the daily's support in membership drives and without taking a stand on the Committee's reason for being. I said that as long as the majority of the Legion believed the sort of junk that was being published in the Committee's monthly, it was better that the junk be set down in black and white where it could be refuted than that the Legionnaires should gather around in little groups and brood over it.

An odd development from that was that the editors of the Americanism monthly (who were also cochairmen of the Committee) reached the conclusion that they had more in common with me than with the middle-roading daily. Finally one of them called me one day and invited me to meet him and his coworker for coffee.

We met in a neighborhood cafe that had a bar partially walled off in one corner and booths along one side of the larger room, the sort of place that is the nearest thing to the neighborhood tavern that the mores of southwest Missouri permit. When I got there, my hosts were ensconced in a booth, drinking coffee. They were personable, well-dressed young men, distinguishable from the usual run of my associates chiefly by their more intense manner.

In that conspiratorial atmosphere, we did discover that we had a few common antipathies, such as the Eisenhower Administration and political pussyfooting in general. But they failed to see that the theory on which I based my defense of their right to free speech also covered the rights of Howard Fast and the Reverend E. Stanley Jones, a Socialist lecturer whose appearance in Springfield a while earlier had been the subject of one of their denunciations.

I lost any desire to set them straight when one of them said to me in a friendly way, and as if out of pure curiosity, "I guess you people have your plans all ready to take over. What would they do with somebody like you, put you on propaganda?"

On the off-chance that he was serious, and really thought that I was in on the inner circles of some powerful apparatus, I chose not to wreck his illusions. I thought what an exciting fantasy life he must be leading, especially at that moment, when he had had the audacity to stage a confrontation with the enemy in the form of a friendly coffee break.

So I played along. I said, "Well, naturally. This is not going to be like the Army, you know. No square pegs in round holes."

Of course I wound up the conversation as fast as I could after that. Regrettably, I am almost as ignorant about the essentials of Communism as I am about those of music. All I know of either I learned from my father when I was a child, and as a Debs Socialist, my father was vociferously against the Communists, whom he called the Bolshevyekies. I gathered that what he held most against them was that they were for throwing bombs, while he was a dedicated pacifist. I have never even so much as seen, in person, anyone I knew to be a Communist, much less plotted with a group of them.

Nevertheless, during the McCarthy years, and especially when I was laying myself open to attack by the local Red-hunters, I was grateful that pure luck had saved me from having become at least a Fronter during my college years. The only reason I didn't send a dollar to a peace group that advertised for members in the magazines I was reading was that I didn't have the dollar to spare. The advertisement featured a touching picture of a mother bending over her dying son, and it listed as sponsors every American writer whose work had any appeal for me at all. I felt very guilty at the time about putting my stomach before my conscience, but I have occasionally since felt very superior for having resisted an appeal that took in many older and supposedly wiser persons. The truth is, though, that it was just pure luck.

My journalistic defense of liberal viewpoints has convinced a few other of my fellow citizens that I'm a flaming Red. One of them, the wife of a leading citizen, told me to my face at a country-club cocktail party one evening that she knew I was a Communist. However, I thought that she, like the Legion Americanists, was surprisingly amiable about it under the circumstances, and, as usual, I was amiable right back. Instead of offending me, people who make that charge continue to fascinate me. I can't help speculating that the idea that a person who moves among them, lives in the same neighborhood, shops at the same stores, pays the same income tax, goes to some of the same parties, and banks at the same banks is (at the same time, and stripped down) a foreign agent

—that this idea must be one of the spiciest they permit themselves. When I'm presented with the opportunity, I always feel at the moment that it would be cruel to deprive them of their exciting fantasy.

The most virulent animosity I have ever stirred up among readers of what I have written for local consumption has been among ardent lovers of cats and of Senator Barry Goldwater and of the segregationists. In fact I have reason to suspect that the first two groups overlapped, although the cat-lovers, on the whole, responded more in sorrow than in anger, while the response of the Goldwater lovers was weighted in the other direction. I considered my remarks on both cats and the senator rather mild— I had no strong feelings about either one of them, taking them as individuals. The worst I said about cats was that I was indifferent to them, sensing that they had about the same attitude toward me. But then I rashly added that if all the cats in the world dropped dead overnight, my life would go on about the same as usual. That addendum appalled a small but vocal group of my readers to the point that a few of them called me, in tears, vowing never to read another word that I wrote. A Goldwater-lover, by contrast, neatly clipped a column I had written questioning the senator's right to blame the nation's loose morals on the Democrats, then this reader apparently used the clipping for toilet paper, after which he mailed it to me—unsigned.

A few of our town's violent segregationists have proved to be more unforgiving than even the McCarthy-, the cat-, or the Goldwater-lovers. The Negro population in Springfield at the time of the Supreme Court school-integration decision was less than 1 per cent of the total, and many of the Negro families are among the oldest and most

stable in the county. I pointed some of these things out
in news stories and in editorials ridiculing our civic leaders for pretending that they had a racial problem comparable to those in the big cities and in the South.

But the Negro families with the oldest Greene County
lineage are the descendants of slaves owned by the forebears of the oldest white families in the county, and
neither group has ever quite recovered from the attitudes
that relationship spawned. Integration views and political views still divide along Civil War lines.

I myself spring from the redneck Republican contingent, my father having been the only political maverick
on either side of the family. When I was old enough to
vote for the first time and said I was going to vote for
Roosevelt, my grandmother Williams said, "*You* can't
vote for a Democrat. Both your grandfathers fought
against them Democrats."

I had never seen a Negro until the morning after we
moved to Neosho, when I was five years old, and went
into a restaurant to eat breakfast. When the cook set our
plates of eggs and bacon on the shelf in back for the
waiter, I said, "Oh look! That lady is black."

Grace shushed me with a frown and whispered, "That's
a Negro." And then I couldn't eat my breakfast.

All I knew then about Negroes was that if a child let
himself get beyond a certain danger point of dirtiness he
would become one (pronounced "nigger"). I naturally
thought that food cooked by anyone who had gone beyond that limit would be highly unsanitary, to say the
least. Besides having heard the word in warnings ("If you
don't wash them face and hands you're just goin' to turn
into a nigger"), I was also acquainted with it in "nigger-
flipper," a plaything for shooting small rocks at birds; in

"nigger-toe," a Brazil nut; and in "sweatin' like a nigger dilection" (the last word of which phrase, as I learned before I quit saying it myself, was really a contraction of "at election").

After we had left the restaurant that morning, my father belatedly told me about the unchangeableness of skin color, but it took me a long time to cure myself of the effects of my infant ignorance, and I couldn't swear that I have ever done so altogether, though I would rather die than consciously let it influence my conduct.

The next Negro I saw up close after that became my friend and playmate for a couple of weeks. That was after we had moved to Chitwood and I had been invited by some ex-Polk-County neighbors to stay at their farm during blackberry season and pick and can wild blackberries for our family. Across the road from our ex-neighbor's place, there was a small, neat model farm belonging to a Joplin businessman who used it as an occasional weekend retreat. A Negro couple lived in the house the year round, as caretakers. They had a pretty little daughter, Tiny Doll, who was a year or so younger than I. I had seen other Negroes at a distance—on the streets of Joplin and at the city park—and I had come to think of them as strictly urban creatures, so what impressed me most about Tiny Doll was that she was a good horseback rider. I could ride a horse too, but I considered it only a rather uncomfortable means of getting from one place to another, and I preferred a car. Tiny Doll rode horses for fun.

Mrs. Rowland wouldn't let Tiny Doll go blackberry-picking with me, among the briers, the chiggers, and the snakes. And she seemed rather to disapprove of our even playing together. Bessie Copeland, my hostess, was equally unenthusiastic about the association, and my feeling at the time was that a racial clannishness was behind the adult coolness. But now I surmise that there was a mutual feeling of social superiority. To the Rowlands, the poor hillbillies across the road were white trash, while the Copelands felt the superiority of their color, their own ignorance and poverty aside.

As a columnist and editor sympathetic to the aims of the local NAACP, I was able to affect the income of certain die-hard local segregationists, or at least they feared I might, and this is the most unforgivable thing a gadfly can do. The anonymous letters and phone calls I received from rabid segregationists were the only ones that ever really depressed me very much.

On the other hand, I have acquired support from surprising quarters because of certain stands I have taken. The most distinguished Baptist minister in town, the one Jewish rabbi, and the one Catholic monseigneur all commended me privately for what I had to say in defense of a junior high school science teacher who was fired for telling his class, in reply to a point-blank question from a student, that he wasn't sure there was a God. What I had said was to the effect that no teacher should be fired for expressing his honest opinion on religion, or anything else, if he was asked for it, and that junior high students were old enough to survive the knowledge that there are respectable people who hold views that do not coincide with those of their parents. I could only assume that the various commendatory churchmen felt that I was with them on this because I wasn't against them.

The prospective female gadfly must, of course, be prepared to forgo a regular social life among the country-club set, but her company will be sought by the intellectuals and Upper Bohemians, and they are much more fun. The least attractive characteristic of many of the latter, in fact, is that they mind so much not being socially accepted by the country-clubbers. It is saddening that name-dropping among distinguished professors so often consists in references to the rich industrialists or doctors they know, and that so many of them would consider it a greater honor to be elected to the board of the chamber of commerce or of the local country club than to be awarded almost any scholastic honor. Unfortunately, such people can never be convinced that the topmost people among the group they envy usually return the sentiment.

Among our town's three or four richest and most socially distinguished men, the one I admired most for his character and intellect implied to me once that he regarded his country-club dues as in the nature of an eleemosynary expense—his contribution toward providing wholesome recreation for the town's Four Hundred. Nor did he exclude the unending game of striving to rise within the social set's pecking order from among the wholesome activities a country club provides. "In a group like that," he told me once, "snobbery is one of the most potent socializing forces." He thought that centrifugal action would inevitably bring the best to the top, even in a small-town high-society group, and that it was good exercise for the rest to concentrate their attention on trying to make themselves acceptable to those at the top, seeing that they had nothing more momentous to strive toward. He said he knew a dozen hillbilly girls who had married successful men and would die happy because they had thereafter managed eventually to make their way into the top social circles at the country club.

I said, "You know, I believe I could make it." And he

gave me the most reassuring compliment I had had up
to then, as well as a lesson in values, by laughing with
genuine glee and asking me derisively, "Do you really
think you could make the big leap into that rarefied atmosphere?" With that response, he dimmed forever the
fleeting glitter that social prominence sometimes flashed
at me, and helped to free me for the pursuit of fearless
local journalism.

While I was developing my role as the voice of opposition at home, I had continued with free-lancing and had
settled on a specialty for my *Post-Dispatch* reviews and
articles and for the pieces I was trying on magazine editors. The switch I had made as a child from the rural to
the urban Ozark dialect had caused me to focus my attention on American speech habits. I at first studied and
wrote about dialect and I went naturally from that to
the English language in general. A piece I wrote on
English usage, with the "light touch," which was published in *Harper's* "After Hours" department, was the
first one I sold to a national magazine. By that time, I
was also writing a short bimonthly column on usage for
the *Post-Dispatch*'s Sunday culture pages, and for this I
was studying all the extant dictionaries and books on
usage and language in general, while, at the same time,
making my own conclusions from firsthand evidence. I
sold pieces on the subject to several other magazines—
sending them out cold—and one of those, a "light-touch"
piece that appeared in *TV Guide*, entitled (by the editors) "TV Talks Good Like a Medium Should," eventually
got me in on the fringes of professional, academic linguistics and lexicography.

The late Professor Porter G. Perrin read the *TV Guide*
piece and wrote to me about collaborating with him on a

revision of a popular textbook on usage he had written. I accepted the invitation and devoted most of my time to the book for the next two years. For that project, I started a systematic collection of words and phrases in context (called "cites" in the trade), and by the end of the two years I had a file of about sixty thousand of them. When I was winding up my part of the usage book, the editor of a dictionary published by the firm that also publishes the usage book came to Springfield to look over my files and then offered me a nice sum for permission to copy the cites for the dictionary. He also hired me to continue collecting, with the original copies of new cites to go to the dictionary and eventually gave me another job—as consulting editor of the dictionary.

I had been working on the usage textbook for about a year when the controversial third edition of Webster's New International Dictionary came out. I wrote a favorable review of it for the *Post-Dispatch*—the first favorable comment on it to be published in a major periodical, as it turned out—and later another favorable piece about it in *Harper's* magazine. I thus got in on the fringes of what has proved to be the most prolonged and heated academic and literary battle of the twentieth century up to now. But though the reviews and some other pieces I have written on the dictionary have been reprinted several times, and though the Library of Congress requested the original manuscript of the *Harper's* piece, my obviously female name has not been mentioned in print, so far as I know, in the continuing (all-male) debate that the original reception of the dictionary instantly set off. I attribute this omission to pure absent-mindedness, a mental lacuna that has no doubt had Freudian origins.

It has really been a very strange debate and it has

finally undermined my belief in the intelligence, the judgment, or the good faith of many men whom I had theretofore stood in awe of. I will have to go further and confess that it has made me suspicious of all opinions and inferences, no matter how seemingly well-founded or how brilliant and well-informed their promulgators. If so many errors and misconceptions about something so available for examination as the English language can be advanced by the acknowledged experts, who can tell what fantasies are being fobbed off on us as the truth by the experts in more recondite fields?

When I first began studying and writing about current English, I went on the assumption that the rules I had learned in school covered all phases of its grammar, syntax, and vocabulary, and that those rules were immutable. While I was still of that innocent persuasion, I read a composite review by Dwight Macdonald in the *New Yorker* of three books on American English. I had admired all the other essays by Macdonald I had read, and I was so elated to find that his views of the three language books were the same as mine that I sent him clippings of the reviews I had written on the same books for the *Post-Dispatch*. He wrote back complimenting my reviews for both their style and their content and urging me to do a book on current American usage myself. We exchanged a few more friendly notes, and shortly after that I got into an equally friendly correspondence with Jacques Barzun, with whom I felt a similar linguistic rapport. But as soon as I actually began writing material for a book on usage and doing the necessary research, I lost all my childish faith in the applicability of the traditional rules of grammar to the English that is in actual use.

Shortly after my apostasy began, I got an assignment

from the *Saturday Evening Post* to do a profile of Professor Charles Carpenter Fries, the antitraditionalist grammarian at the University of Michigan, whom Jacques Barzun had denounced in a book of his I had admiringly reviewed. My conversations with Dr. Fries convinced me once and for all that he was right and Dr. Barzun wrong.

(The *Saturday Evening Post* editor with whom I was dealing wanted to rewrite the profile, but, already skeptical of the linguistic competence of editors, I demurred. The *Saturday Review* finally bought it—for a fraction of the *SEP*'s fee.)

It happened that my two distinguished correspondents later wrote reviews of Webster III (as we insiders came to refer to the new Webster's unabridged dictionary among ourselves) that were among the most notorious attacks on it, Macdonald's appearing in the *New Yorker*, and Barzun's in the *American Scholar*.

The editors of the *New Republic*, the *Nation*, and the New York *Times* joined them; and Edmund Wilson, America's foremost literary critic, although not singling out Webster III specifically, has expressed similar sentiments regarding the primacy of "rules" over usage as a guide to language correctness. Since language, among all the topics these leading American critics and editors discuss, is the one I know most about, and since I know that they are demonstrably wrong about it, I have naturally become skeptical of most of their premises.

Why do I not entertain the possibility that the distinguished critics and editors are right, and that those of us who accept usage as the only criterion of correctness are wrong? Because it is obvious that the language of Chaucer became the language of Shakespeare, and the language of Shakespeare that of Dwight Macdonald and Jacques Barzun through the gradual obsolescence of "rules" from one period to another, and that these rules were made obsolete through being flouted in a constantly evolving consensus by the speakers of the language as a whole.

The most easily demonstrable proof that the acknowledged experts on English usage, whether liberal or conservative, are self-deluded about the inexorable erosion of usage on rules is to quote them against themselves. I once took *A Dictionary of Contemporary American Usage,* by Bergen and Cornelia Evans—who I then thought were on my side—to an adult education class in English I was teaching, to read four passages that applied to questions that had arisen in class. Coincidentally, of the two pairs I read successively, the first seemed to my students (embarrassingly for me) to contradict the second in both cases. The first was on *overall,* which I had accused my students of overusing. About this word the Evanses say, among other things: "It is commonly misused as a synonym for any number of more precise words . . . As Collins has observed, in most uses *overall* is at best an inelegant variation, a mere manifestation, that is, of a desire for variety even at the cost of precision and clarity." The very next passage I chose to read was on *commas* and I began at this point: "The best overall piece of advice on the use of commas is given by H. W. Fowler." Next, to demonstrate the power of usage to change the status of even obscene words, I had selected the Evanses' amusing comment on the word *poppycock.* Noting that it "parallels a vulgar and unprintable expletive," they add that it has nevertheless come to be "particularly favored, as an expression of disgust, by the prim." Then, while my students were still laughing at the prim innocents of this world, I turned to the Evanses' discussion of *poetic diction* to bolster my arguments against fancy language, and read: "Long forgotten now as a poet but deserving some remembrance as the supreme perpetrator of this particular kind of polysyllabic poppycock is Dr. John Armstrong. . . ."

But this is a trap that lies in the path of any writer who presumes to make a flat statement about any feature of English whose status is uncertain enough to be discussed in the first place. Nearly all the solecisms that teachers and editors are harping on here in this last half of the twentieth century were among those that the first systematic grammarians of the English language were already trying to rout from our tongue in the eighteenth century. The very longevity of the locutions would be proof to anybody but a native-English-speaking grammarian that they are permanent features of the language; or as permanent, that is, as anything else in the language is likely to be.

I restrict this comment on grammarians to those for whom English is a native language because others, approaching English with an unprejudiced eye, can see it as any of the rest of us see any foreign language. As outsiders trying to learn French, for example, we do not question the fact that the real French language is the language used by the French speakers we hear, and the French writers we read. We are interested only, peripherally, if at all, in the views of the French Academy as to what is "incorrect" French. Our purpose is simply to learn to speak French in a way that would least differentiate us from the Frenchmen of whatever class we may hope to mingle with.

And that is essentially the attitude we have as we constantly modify our own language—though that is usually an unconscious process. I happen to have a mental peculiarity—one of several—that makes me continuously word-conscious. I automatically analyze the language I speak or write, or hear or read. But this peculiarity does not make the person who has it more censorious of his own or other people's language. It has just the opposite effect. We eventually learn that almost every speaker of English who is physically and mentally normal follows all the important rules of the language unerringly; those who deviate are usually simply following another rule, as when they are speaking another dialect.

The habitual word-watcher is therefore not very likely to be inspired to write a grammar or handbook in which he tells other native speakers of his language how to use it properly. His preoccupation causes him to find his language more interesting than most people do—or perhaps it's the other way around—but it interests him as the stars interest an astronomer. He wants to know about it and to enlighten others, but he doesn't delude himself that he could change the parts of it he doesn't like, even if he wanted to.

All authors of prescriptive grammars and handbooks on English usage sooner or later reveal themselves in their own works as having a faulty ear. All of them, including H. W. Fowler, whose *Modern English Usage* is still the purist's bible after forty years, violate several of their own dicta when they are involved in making points about something else, thus demonstrating that no one is immune to the effects of usage, and undermining their whole case. (Fowler uses *beside* for *besides*, writes *com-*

monsense as one word, and says *as with* for *as of*, among other things.)

This sort of thing does not teach such types not to lay down the law, however, or persuade them to admit that the effect of usage is too insidious to be evaded. They would rather guiltily admit that they themselves sometimes forget to observe a certain "rule" than to admit that the rule doesn't exist. More than once in his usage dictionary, Eric Partridge arrives at a "rule" through the application of logic, then meekly admits that he, and practically everybody else, has been ignorantly violating it.

Such demonstrations of the fallibility of English-usage authoritarians—and I could expand them indefinitely—do not persuade literary critics or editors that language prescriptivism is only an exercise in futility, however. In practice, they constantly flout many of the dicta of the lexicographers and the grammarians they profess allegiance to, no doubt because they are blissfully unaware of about ninety per cent of them. But they apparently have a deep emotional need to be sure that certain impressive volumes of authoritative rulings on the rights and wrongs of language are there at their elbows to appeal to.

I think this odd literary and editorial mental quirk goes back to the schoolroom—if not still farther back to the Jungian racial memory of the medicine man that I have discussed. Most people become writers and editors in the first place because of the early gratification they felt at their superior skill in manipulating words according to teacher's directions. To admit the irrevocable departure from their lives of the stern taskmaster who first flattered them at the expense of their less verbally facile classmates, and who occasionally satisfied their masochis-

tic longings by making pedantic and illogical, though—
for them—easily mastered rulings, would leave an unen-
durable void.

The pertinence of this editorial state of mind to my
current literary activities lies in the fact that my usage
research has almost disqualified me from writing for general publication on the topic about which I am best
informed. The things I learn that strike me as most interesting are things that editors would rather not know, and
certainly prefer that the public should not know.

8

Of course a person who has to explain why he has written a memoir probably shouldn't have written one in the first place, but I regard what I have written here as more in the nature of a case history, and my reasons for writing it are therefore pertinent as a part of the record.

The uniqueness that H. L. Mencken saw in me as the speaker of an illiterate dialect who became a scholar of dialects is genuine, as far as I have been able to discover.

There are good reasons for this: most experts who write on dialects—as on anything else—are men, and most boys very early acquire an attitude toward language that precludes them from regarding their own as a proper subject for critical observation. They consider their variety of English, which is also, perforce, the English of their parents, their friends, and their neighbors, as good as anybody else's, so long as it serves its purpose—that is, so long as it is generally understood. When teachers in school reject it, not because they don't understand it but because they regard it as not proper, boys instinctively react by rejecting not only the teacher's manner of speech, but teachers, as a group, and school in general. Judging

them by their emphasis on the alteration of nonconform-
ing speech habits, lower-class boys soon sense that teachers are less interested in imbuing them with useful
knowledge than in acculturating them into the middle
class, and there are few boys who will willingly submit
to being acculturated into any class, especially one with
more constricting folkways than their own. Thus the typical lower-class boy goes to school for only as long as he
has to, all the while passively, or actively, resisting its
pressures to conform, and then he drops out.

The only men that most lower-class boys regularly hear
using "good grammar" are not men they want to look
upon as models. In the Ozarks, for example, they are
such citified, white-collar types as agricultural and insurance agents, and school superintendents and high
school principals. And even among the latter two types,
the most numerous and the most popular are men who
have come up through the ranks by way of coaching
athletics, or teaching mathematics or chemistry, not by
teaching English. They have been able to get by with
making only small gestures toward speech conformity.
I know a former principal of the Bolivar high school,
originally a coach, who says "I tuck it," and "them cab-
bages," and who never did eschew any of his childhood
speech habits except for avoiding "ain't," "knowed," "I
seen," and "I done." The "isn't's," "knew's" and "I did's"
of these types sound especially foppish when they are
pronounced in their unalterable hillbilly accent and intonation, anyway, a fact that is not lost on their possible
young emulators. (Seen and saw are used interchange-
ably in natural Ozark, so the "I saw's" are less jarring than
the other "proper" forms when spoken in the Ozark
twang.)

The normal male Ozarker feels that speech is a physiological function, like digestion, and that it is unseemly to dwell on its processes or to call undue attention to one's own or other people's style of executing it. I think that the Ozarker's impulse to speak in whatever way seems most natural and easy for him is essentially an aristocratic one; he shares it with, among other speakers of English, the British upper class. This is the reason the two groups have in common Jessica Mitford's British-U vocabulary, both groups preferring the plain, or Anglo-Saxon word to the euphemistic or Latinate: false teeth instead of dentures; looking-glass instead of mirror; rich instead of wealthy; fat instead of heavy-set. The distaste for making a fuss about speaking extends to exerting too much energy at it and accounts for the peculiar monotony of the vowel sounds in both the Ozark and the British-U dialects even though their pronunciation is so dissimilar. The Britisher forms his mouth into a vertical oval when he starts to speak and keeps it that way until he is done, so that everything he says comes out "haw." The Ozarker elongates his mouth into a horizontal line, or rather, he just leaves it as nearly closed as possible while still being audible, so that everything comes out "hee."

The few Ozark boys who do eventually yield on a few points of grammar and syntax do so for vocational purposes—because they aim to become agricultural or insurance agents or high school principals. Nothing in the world except the aspiration to become a radio or television announcer will make any male abandon his native accent and intonation, however. I have heard college English professors address their fellows at Modern Language Association meetings on the subject of dialects while using accents of their own that were almost unintelligible. And of course we all know the inflexibility of presidents and senators, whose regional lingo is left untouched by decades in Washington and years of junketing abroad.

Lower-class boys who adopt middle-class grammar and syntax usually go through life feeling rather sheepish about this abandonment of principle, and prefer to forget it. To expect them to discuss it is like expecting a castrato to talk about his operation. They are certainly not likely to use their linguistic metamorphosis as a basis for their life work.

Girls, on the other hand, learn before they ever start to school that they can win the sort of adult acceptance that falls naturally to boys only by being good—that is, by conforming to adult expectations. By the age of six, they are used to having their natural impulses aborted, and they are all set to be obedient and talk as teacher tells them to. They soon become, therefore, "good in English," in teacher's opinion. Most of the editors of Ozarks high school papers, which are subsidized by the school boards as training grounds for journalists, are girls. (The teachers who appoint editors have obviously never pondered the significance of the fact that all real editors are male.) Given enough inducement, girls will even drop their native accents. For example, any woman in public life who talked with the unmitigated regional accents of any of our last four presidents would be considered an inconsiderate ass—at least by other women.

Not being put off by the teacher's meddling with their language, girls easily go on to swallow the whole lower-middle-class outlook, at least as teachers see it. There are dozens of lower-class-rural Ozarks girls who pass docilely into the urban lower-middle class every year, most of them having themselves been transformed into teachers on the way. In the process they lose the wholesome view, acquired from their fathers, that speech is better not tampered with. They acquire instead an itch to tamper with everybody's—wholesale. The linguists are right about such girls—they do reject their origins, though which of the two they emotionally abandon first, their native dialect or its milieu, is a moot question. But those who, like me, spoke the most outré dialect (low-class rural) are content to have made it into the lower-middle class; they gratefully stop there. They become altogether very good and very proper. And, in their docile conforming, they are likely to have lost their zest, their courage, and their creativity. They consequently feel no need to explore beyond what they learned from their teachers and from their books to discover what really is permissible conduct for free human beings, whether linguistically, morally, or ethically. None of that group who are my contemporaries is therefore likely to contribute anything novel to the study of sociolinguistics, and none has, so far as I know, or so far as H. L. Mencken knew, before me.

That leaves me.

There is so much of my early life that strikes me as squalidly depressing that it has given me no special pleasure to rake any of it over, but editors and other writers have finally pushed me into it. The hints about my peculiar origins that they have found in other things I have written have piqued their curiosity. In letters rejecting my book and article ideas, editors often advise me to get down to bedrock and disclose once and for all how I got this way—as one editor put it, "how a hillbilly girl got to the point where she could beat the experts in her field at their own game."

(The game he referred to was American English, and it is only the nonacademic editors who profess to see the superiority of my writing on the subject to those of the Ph.D.s in the field. Few of the Ph.D.s themselves concede it and I often have my own doubts. What chiefly detracts from my authenticity, in the opinion of the scholars, is that I came at my field by the journalistic route. This has also ruled out H. L. Mencken forever, on both the American language and American literature, in the opinion of the academic writers. They dismiss his opinions on either by referring to him as "the journalist, H. L. Mencken." I think they have some justification for this, in Mencken's case, but I still will not admit that a Ph.D. is an indispensable prerequisite for a writer on either language or literature.)

Even a few of the experts who do not admit that I am one of their number have conceded that I have "made a place for myself," or something like that, in their field, and have joined the editors in curiosity as to how and why. So, distasteful as it has been to me on the whole, I am telling. I am a writer by vocation, and, if the most interesting and instructive thing I can write about is my own personal history, I bow to galling circumstance. I console myself that, any other possible merit aside, the document is in the nature of a sociological tract, with special pertinence to sociolinguistics. With the war on poverty in progress and aimed directly at my specific milieu, I may be contributing a bit of otherwise unrecoverable Americana. (I hope so, for purely unselfish reasons.)

According to the statistics on IQs and social adjustment in relation to genetics and culture, I should be a maladjusted moron—an ex-dropout, living on the dole:

broken home, large family, rural, lack of parental encouragement, no religion, no books or other cultural advantages, and, worst of all, a female. I have put down everything that seemed to me pertinent, so that interested poverty warriors may decide for themselves why the statistics don't fit me, hoping they may find their discoveries useful. But I should add, for their information, that my IQ probably hasn't changed much since I left the Joplin slum. It was the second highest in the one junior high school in Joplin before I left Chitwood, according to information a high school teacher later gave me confidentially. It was partly the circumstances of my learning this fact that made it seem more disturbing than reassuring to me. My informant was a teacher I didn't know who sent me word that she had something personal to discuss with me. This was alarming enough in itself and, when I got to her office for the conference, I was still more unsettled. The teacher could have been the model for Chas Addams's chatelaine, except that her Medusa locks were deceptively done up in a demure chignon, which she wore low on her neck. She told me in husky confidential tones that she wanted to help guide me in my high school career. She said that the student with an IQ higher than mine—a handsome boy who was a grade ahead of me (she told me his name)—had become her protégé the year before and that they had established a mutually rewarding relationship. I thanked her and got away as quickly as I could, and I avoided her carefully after that.

Another reason the information failed to reassure me was that I had good reason to suspect that the test didn't mean much. One of my classmates, Charlie Kilburn, had demonstrated in mathematics and chemistry classes a hundred times that he could think faster than I could. Charlie, the archetypal bright kid—short, underweight, myopic—was all brain, and remembering his intellectual feats in the schoolroom is all I have ever needed to allay any suspicions I might have that I might be a genius. I knew then that if the IQ test we took showed me to be brighter than Charlie, something was wrong with the test. And now I have to agree with the critics of IQ tests who charge they are chiefly tests of verbal facility. As for the further charge that they are rigged against the low-class-rural testees, I remember only two words on the test I took—one was *piccolo*, which I naturally didn't know, though my urban peers with whom I discussed the test did, and the other was *pollen*, which I naturally knew and they didn't. An even break there, I thought.

H. L. Mencken, writing in one of his language books about the Appalachian stock from which I spring, noted that not many of them ever diverge from the common (low) level of culture. But he added that they sometimes produce "at somewhat longish intervals, individuals of marked ability—whether by chance adulteries or by some fortunate collocation and effervescence of Mendelian characters is not certain."

I am able to rule out adultery in the case of my own genetic stock, and I have less faith than Mencken in the power of the genes to transmit such characteristics as ambition and an academic bent.

Perhaps some sociolinguist who reads the foregoing account will discover just what it was that drove me out of the hills. If so, I'll be most interested to know.

9

What I had that permitted me to become assimilated while retaining some vestiges of my ego was, I think, a freakish ability to look at myself and at what was happening to me with a certain detachment. Even as I was suffering total heartbreak or despair—or at least not long afterward—I was usually able to see myself, and the other people involved in the events, as if we were all characters in a melodrama. No doubt my having been surfeited with melodrama via those free silent movies and true-confession stories during my urban-slum period immunized me against its effects forever. At any rate I was able to see, at an early age, that my own personal crises and tragedies were of less than earthshaking importance and that my overwrought reactions to them were absurd, from the cosmic view. (That knowledge, I must confess, never has cured me of a susceptibility to momentary seizures of deeply felt self-pity.)

But I realize that such detachment *is* freakish in a child, and that more normal children who are ground through the sort of acculturation mill that I chose to subject myself to are likely either to resist or to emerge emotionally mangled. Now that the country is gearing up to process all low-class children in a manner roughly comparable to the way in which I processed myself, it behooves those who are taking the responsibility to give some serious thought to their methods, and to the end product they desire.

Among native-born Americans, the hillbilly and the Negro children are the most recalcitrantly unacculturated and are likely to remain so for some years. Most of them will, no doubt, eventually submit to some improved method that is yet to be devised for socializing them; our society will not tolerate their remaining as an undigested lump in its large urban maw much longer. And the schools will necessarily play the leading role in any such successful socializing process.

The first purpose of the schools is to establish literacy, and this can be done best in all cases, and solely in some, by teachers who have discarded all the old notions about the nature of language. A child will learn faster to read and to write, and he will always write better, if the written language is first presented to him as merely a visible representation of actual speech. For a child just acquiring literacy, this notion can be conveyed best in transcriptions of his own speech. The child says something; the teacher writes it on the board; everybody reads it.

But what if the child says something like, "I ain't saw no flars yet this spring"? If the teacher stops to reprimand him for his grammar and pronunciation and then writes, "I haven't seen any flowers yet this spring," she is not only inhibiting the child at a crucial point in his understanding of the nature of writing, but she is also affronting him by vague implications that he (and his family and friends) are guilty of some undefined kind of misbehavior. To offset these negative aspects of her response, she is not even realizing the positive one of eliminating the child's low-class language habits. *Ain't,* and the double negative, and the indiscriminate use of *saw* and *seen* have all survived three hundred years of violent opposition by the schoolmarms of America.

Though my own ancestors left the Appalachians more than a hundred and twenty years ago, the first non-Ozarker I ever met who talked just as I had as a child was a high school graduate from Mount Airy, North Carolina, near where the first Reeds settled in the late seventeenth century. Even though I was already a student of dialects at the time and aware of the origin of my own, I was astounded at the hardiness it had shown by remaining so nearly identical with its Eastern branch for so long. GIs from the Ozarks were also struck by this phenomenon; many have told me that they instantly recognized their kinship with the good old mountain boys from the Southeast as soon as they heard them speak. Teachers and other language purists who are concerned that the "permissiveness" of lexicographers and grammar teachers will bring on linguistic anarchy should be reassured by this evidence that a language can survive even a concerted and determined effort to eradicate it, but they will probably not be. It may at least, though, convince the teacher who shrinks from writing "ain't" on the board that whether or not she does will not have much effect on its longevity.

(As for the pronunciation, the transcription of the low-class "flars" as "flowers" is innocuous. There are at least half a dozen socially approved ways of pronouncing *flowers,* and everybody is free to read the word as a representation of his own version of it. In this respect, English writing resembles Chinese ideography.)

Suppose, instead, that the teacher writes down the child's actual words, and then perhaps the approved version, explaining that the second is the one used in books and by some speakers, without indicating that the first is in any way inferior. What harm would she be doing? She is no more likely, by this schoolroom exercise, to have a permanent effect on the speech habits of the children who are used to saying "I haven't any" than she is on the habits of those who say "I ain't seen no." And "ain't" *is* an English word with a long history which has the virtue of being phonetically spelled, and which is frequently seen in print. There is no real reason why a teacher should find writing it on the blackboard, in a sentence uttered from his heart by an innocent child, a traumatic experience.

In England it has always been taken for granted that low-class children will emerge from their bout of enforced schooling with their low-class dialects intact, even though, one must suppose, the instruction is carried on in U-British, just as if the pupils *were* expected to acquire the prestige dialect for everyday use, as their American counterparts are. (The British U-dialect is sometimes identified as "public school"—meaning "private school"—from the fact that it is only in those cradles of Establishment culture that a mastery of so-called Standard British is insisted upon, or usually acquired.) The fictional assumption on which both British and American schools operate—that they are transforming the speech habits of their lower-class pupils and must therefore insist upon use of standard English in teaching and learning every discipline—sets up an extra barrier in the paths of the very children who are least well equipped to hurdle it.

But, back to our American first-grader and his low-class sentence—all American children will eventually learn from observing the speech habits of a Will Rogers, or a Dick Gregory, or of some Gary Cooper type cowboy, that there *are* people worthy of their esteem who say *ain't*, so why shouldn't they learn it early when their acceptance of the fact will be of some benefit to their less fortunate age peers?

Before any teacher can bring herself to write a sentence in low-class dialect on the board without betraying her inner distaste, however, she will have had to have done some serious thinking about the right of every child—and every adult for that matter—to be left with his dignity and his self-respect, his poverty and ignorance notwithstanding. When enough teachers do arrive at that point, schools will become more attractive to the children who need them most, in all subjects. But it is most important that the child's natural facility for language—which even the most backward savage commands to a marvelous degree when he is compared to the next highest primate in the evolutionary scale—should not be thwarted.

After a child has learned to set down his spontaneous thoughts in writing, and has thus made the transfer from spoken to written, even if that takes all his elementary school years, is soon enough for him to begin to learn the prestige dialect. Educators who insist on the use of "correct" grammar from the first defend their position by pointing out that a low-class dialect will hamper a pupil in the rest of his school career and in job-hunting later. But the first handicap will be removed when *all* teachers acquire an enlightened view of social dialects, which shouldn't take long. To educate employers on the point will take longer, but they will eventually learn. Those coming out of enlightened schoolrooms will, of course, start out with a sophisticated linguistic view. Anyway, teachers are inclined to overestimate the amount of linguistic persnickitiness that prevails among employers. Those who are hiring baseball or football players, or truck drivers or bricklayers are likely to find a too-careful diction faintly repulsive in a job applicant. Their own tones are likely to be, in fact, something less than perfectly pear-shaped.

Recognizing the extra hurdle that their language sets up for the children of native American immigrants to the large cities, some urban school systems have already started attacking the problem in new ways, though some of these are quite unrealistic. An English supervisor in one big-city school system, where the unassimilated pupils are mostly Negro children from the rural South, has, for example, written a book for the use of the teachers of high school English. She tells the teachers that Negro children can be motivated to switch dialects if they are told that they will not be able to blend into the middle class until they do so. The children are so well aware of a less easily eradicable block to this goal that they must find the supervisor's argument as laughable as it is. Those who are taken in by it—and at best that is likely to be only few of the more tractable girls—will find that the damage they do to their acceptability among their own in-group, back in their ghettos, will probably not be compensated by an equal improvement in their status in their target group.

The supervisor suggested as another argument for speech conformity that the teachers tell the Negro-dialect speakers that their low-class speech arouses hostility in its hearers. But the Negro child who chooses Dick Gregory or Louie Armstrong, instead of, say, Ralph Bunche, for his model can see that that argument is patently false.

In this book for English teachers, the supervisor included a list of common expressions that the teachers should aim at eliminating and, alongside those, the "correct" forms. Unfortunately I sent my review copy of her book to a linguist I know, so I can't quote from the lists verbatim, but the following pair is typical: (Wrong) "Man, you really, like, flipped." (Right) "You appear to have become quite excited." In short, any writer in his right mind—or any teacher or employer, for that matter —would recognize the "wrong" list as superior, by all really important linguistic criteria, to the "right" one. Most practicing writers reading the "wrong" list would, in fact, feel an itch to get in among those high-schoolers with a tape recorder to pick up some good samples of colorful conversation. A more telling indication of the wrong-headedness of the supervisor's approach is that many of the words she hoped to weed out—such as *pad, dig, bug, clobber, flip,* and *nary*—have since been picked up by all kinds of writers, or were even then appearing in the works of our best essayists and reviewers.

Such unrealistic attacks on language nonconformity are a waste of valuable time and effort on the part of both teachers and pupils. They are doomed from the start. In fact Dick Gregory's practice of wholeheartedly embracing all the supposed stigmata of his racial group—the fondness for the watermelon and the fatback along with the *ain't*—may represent the direction of the future trend of Negro adaptation, or, rather, refusal to adapt. When it becomes evident to enough educated Negroes that true assimilation is impossible, or not worth the price, more and more of them may come to prefer emphasizing their distinctions. Teachers in the slum schools should certainly learn to understand and respect this impulse too, instead of continuing to regard its manifestations as mere willful disobedience.

The normal Appalachian boy, like his hillbilly Ozarks cousin, resists acculturation from still other impulses. He is of the White-Anglo-Saxon-Protestant (WASP) stock of the dominant American group, and could easily "pass" if he chose to, but the life of the organization man rarely appeals to him, and organization-man language least of all. Hillbilly boys very early become imbued with a restlessness and a recklessness that fits them for pursuits in which some danger and daring is involved, and in which they can win acclaim for individual effort. They succeed as rodeo performers, stock-car drivers, baseball players, and outlaws. (Pretty Boy Floyd and Mickey Mantle both came from the Oklahoma hills.) Their heroes talk hillbilly dialect with no apology. Junior Johnson, the star stock-car-racing driver, for example, says "hit" for "it," and "growed" for "grew," and everything else that teacher tells the little Appalachians not to say.

Oddly enough, the section of the public with whom the adult hillbilly has to deal in the pursuit of his chosen career is more likely to accept his estimate of the worthiness of his style of language than the teachers' estimate. That is, it is generally taken more as a sign of a straightforward, honest, independent, unassuming character than as a mark of slovenliness or vulgarity. There are even many very successful salesmen who speak an unmitigated Appalachian, and not only those who were formerly famous athletes or rodeo performers, and not only in their home territory.

The successful acculturation of poverty-stricken hillbilly and Negro children will require a sympathetic understanding of other phases of low-class culture than the linguistic, of course. For example, low-class children lack the middle-class orientation to group activity, and especially group activity that is controlled by the adult or higher-class power structure. In the one group that the average adult hillbilly aligns himself with—the church—action is usually individual and spontaneous. There is therefore nothing in such groups as the Girl Scouts and the Boy Scouts for the low-class child. They repel him chiefly from his sense that the adults who run them will invade his privacy.

And among other myths that all poverty warriors need to recognize as such are those that poor men dislike working and that poor men's wives, or mistresses, regard having children as a negligible interruption in their carefree days. As for the first myth, industriousness is no respecter of pocketbooks. Like sloth, it cuts across socioeconomic lines and is as likely to appear in its most virulent form in an indigent as in a millionaire. I have known men in both groups who have had an almost pathological urge to be doing something continuously, and other men in both groups who were almost immobilized by a loathing for physical activity. Since I have no taste for watching the latter starve because of their bad luck in not having been born rich, it seems to me only fair that the surplus created by the redundant drive of the compulsive workers be siphoned off to feed them. Their number, in any case, is very small, and their drag on the economy consequently slight. The evolutionary struggle for survival has ensured that most of its survivors do have a drive for productive activity, the real danger in this technological age being that the compulsive producer will swamp us all in his artifacts.

And as for the myth of the women to whom childbearing and infant-tending are such casual matters that they make a career of them for the welfare checks they bring in—that myth will be shown up for what it is as soon as safe legal abortions are provided for all women who request them. That should be soon.